Landmark Visito

The Isle

Marinda Fargher

Marinda Fargher is Manx and has lived all her life on the
Isle of Man in Peel and Maughold and is involved in island
community life. She is a Manx Registered Tourist Guide and
holds an M.A. (Liverpool University) in Manx Studies.

She dedicates this guide book to all who come to visit the
Isle of Man, her family and friends, fellow Tourist Guides
and walkers, her former tutors and fellow students at the
Centre for Manx Studies and all who love the Isle of Man.

She hopes you find it useful.

Published by
Landmark Publishing
Ashbourne Hall, Cokayne Ave, Ashbourne,
Derbyshire DE6 1EJ England

ISLE OF MAN

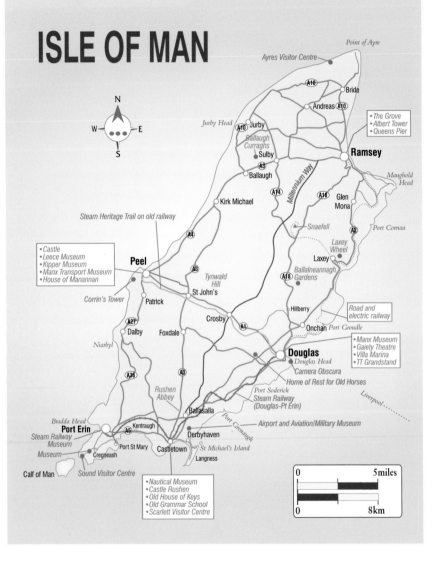

Point of Ayre

Ayres Visitor Centre

A10

Bride

Andreas A10

Jurby Head

A10 Jurby

- The Grove
- Albert Tower
- Queens Pier

Ballaugh
Curraghs

Sulby

A3

Ballaugh

Ramsey

Maughold
Head

A14

Kirk Michael

A18 Glen
Mona

Millennium Way

Snaefell

A2 Port Cornaa

Steam Heritage Trail on old railway

A4

Laxey
Wheel

Laxey

- Castle
- Leece Museum
- Kipper Museum
- Manx Transport Museum
- House of Manannan

Peel

A3

Tynwald
Hill

St John's

Ballalneannagh
A18 Gardens

Corrin's Tower

Patrick

Crosby

Hillberry

Road and
electric railway

A27

Dalby

Foxdale

A1

Onchan Port Groudle

Niarbyl

- Manx Museum
- Gaiety Theatre
- Villa Marina
- TT Grandstand

A36

A3

Douglas

Douglas Head

Camera Obscura

Rushen
Abbey

Home of Rest for Old Horses

Port Soderick
Steam Railway
(Douglas-Pt Erin)

Liverpool

Ballasalla

Airport and Aviation/Military Museum

Port Grenaugh

Bradda Head

Port Erin

Kentraugh

A5

Derbyhaven

Steam Railway
Museum

Museum

Port St Mary

Castletown

St Michael's Island

Cregneash

Langness

Calf of Man

Sound Visitor Centre

- Nautical Museum
- Castle Rushen
- Old House of Keys
- Old Grammar School
- Scarlett Visitor Centre

0	5miles

0	8km

View from Onchan Harbour looking south

Contents

Feature Boxes and Maps

Welcome to
The Isle of Man

Left: Tower of Refuge - Douglas Bay
Opposite: Castle Rushen
Below: The 'Three Legs'

The Isle of Man lies in the centre of the British Isles, but could be its best kept secret! The island is situated in the middle of the Irish Sea, with views of the surrounding coastlines of Ireland, southern Scotland, the north-west coast of England and North Wales.

Top Tips

- Book your travel, accommo-dation and car hire early! (avoid the TT race and race meetings if looking for a quiet break)

- Book your sea or air travel tickets online to save money. See page 84.

- You don't have to stay in Douglas - it's easy to get around.

- You may buy an "explorer" ticket and timetable for island transport in advance of arrival (☎ 01624 662525)

- On arrival, pick up a map and parking disc or "explorer" ticket at the Sea Terminal.

- Ask for the latest "What's On" for local events and details of any road closures.

- Visit the Manx Museum, for an introduction to the island, excellent range of books and Manx crafts admission free.

- Use public transport to explore the countryside - See Chapter 2.

Main attractions:

- Moore's Kipper Musem (Remember to order Kippers to send home!)

- The Manx Musem

- The Steam Train to Peel

- The Electric Tram up Snaefell

- The Laxey Wheel

- Visit a Glen

- The Ayres for birdwatching (also look out for wales and porpoises)

- Peel Castle

- The House of Manannan, Peel

- Close Sartfield Nature Reserve

- Castle Rushen, one of the four Manx National Heritage Sites

It is only half an hour by air from Liverpool, one of the major regional airports which provide links with the island's **Ronaldsway Airport**. The Isle of Man Steam Packet Company operates daily ferry services between **Douglas** and the ports of Liverpool and Heysham, near Lancaster in north-west England – close to motorways and intercity railways. There are regular ferry services to and from Dublin in the Republic of Ireland and Belfast, Northern Ireland in summer. Advance bookings are advised.

The island is a fascinating place to visit. It is not part of the United Kingdom, but an internally self-governing dependent territory of the Crown. The visitor to **Ellan Vannin**, as the Isle of Man is known in Manx Gaelic, will experience the 'Manx' way of life and discover something of its intriguing past. The island has a wealth of fascinating history, folklore and traditions. It has been linked with Manannan, the legendary Celtic sea god, but impor-

tantly it is an ancient Kingdom, proud of its democracy. The Manx Parliament, **Tynwald,** which makes its own laws, was instituted by the Vikings over 1,000 years ago and is the oldest continuous parliament in the world.

The island is 33 miles (52km) long and 12 miles (22km) wide, but the variety of stunning scenery in its area of 227 square miles (572 sq km) is remarkable. There is something naturally spiritual and peaceful about the place. It is wild and unspoilt, a mix of sea and landscape. Areas of open countryside set among green rounded hills are designated of scenic significance while rugged coasts and moorland provide a haven for rare wildlife like hen harriers and choughs.

Bringing your own transport or hiring a vehicle gives you freedom to explore as much as possible of the island, and any point is no more than one hour away. Other options are the excellent public network of buses and the island's original, nostalgic steam and

Vikings and Tynwald dignitories of St. Johns

electric railways, a relaxing way to travel – and to reach the heart of the Manx countryside! For walkers, there are an endless variety of coastal and countryside footpaths, and 24 peaks over 300 metres – the **Snaefell Mountain Railway** climbs to the highest (2,036 ft/621m). Special 'Explorer' tickets allow unlimited travel by road and rail, but you won't have to travel far from a town or village to reach the huge areas of hill land open for public rambling, explore a remote valley, look out over a dramatic coastline or discover an enchanting glen.

Accommodation ranges from the best centrally-located hotels in Douglas to the selection of guesthouses offering bed and breakfast to walkers attempting the island's coastal footpath **'Raad ny Foillan'** ('Road of the Gull'). Campsites provide another option, and sheltered harbours host visiting yachts from around the Irish Sea.

The heartbeat of the island is its sense of national identity, its independent spirit, its 'Manxness'. The population of about 80,000, many born on the island, appreciate the excellent quality of life. The island has its own flag, the **'Three Legs'**, and is known for the **TT motorbike races**, **Manx cats** and the famous **Manx kippers** which may be posted home to friends and family; but look for what makes it different. In addition to its own language and government, the island has its own stamps, phonecards and currency. You can use British sterling currency to buy your postcards, but you will need Manx stamps to post them!

The island's thriving economy, based on its growth as an international business centre and glimpsed in its busy capital, Douglas, contrasts with its unhurried pace of life centred on its many small, mainly rural communities. Each has its own distinctive character – small shops selling quality local produce, cafés, pubs and churches, where people know one another. A Manx expression is '*traa-dy-liooar*', meaning 'time enough'. The island's culture embraces equally the excitement of 'the races', when the island is invaded by thousands of enthusiasts for the annual road-racing festival, and the strong community atmosphere of village fairs, agricultural shows and traditional Celtic music and dance festivals.

The Isle of Man's history and culture are presented at heritage sites throughout the island by Manx National Heritage as the **'Story of Mann'**, a story which begins at the **Manx Museum** in Douglas and unfolds as you discover what makes the Isle of Man so special. All these attractions, some with quality shops and tearooms, can be reached by public transport. National Trust membership tickets are accepted and discounted site passes may be obtained. In addition, fascinating local and specialist museums cover topics ranging from transport to aviation history and kippers!

There is plenty to explore, on and off the beaten track. You will be pleasantly surprised to find many of the island's ancient churches and interesting churchyards open. Or you may wish to sample the Manx beer whilst enjoying a traditional music session in a local pub. By the way, don't forget to greet the 'little people' at the **Fairy Bridge**!

9

Geology

The name 'Man' is thought to come from a word meaning 'mountain'. The story of the Isle of Man began hundreds of millions of years ago when its rocks were formed from sediments deposited on the seabed. The movement of continents folded these sandstones and mudstones into a chain of mountains, which would form the island's green hills and moors. At **Niarbyl**, on the west coast, you can stand with your feet on different rocks from separate continents!

The Manx hills lie like a backbone extending from north-east to south-west. Between these hills lie well-defined valleys which provide endless changes of scenery. A central valley running across the island from Douglas to Peel and dividing the uplands is thought to represent an ancient fault.

A variety of rocks can be seen along the coast, where spectacular geological formations are exposed, and in buildings around the island. The red sandstone at **Peel**, used in the castle and other buildings, gives the town a very different character from **Castletown**, where the local grey limestone predominates in the castle and town and where volcanic rock, pillow lava, dolerite dykes and fossils can be found nearby on the shores.

The island's northern plain is thought of as a 'gift of the ice age', created by glacial deposits such as clay, sands and gravels which are also valued by the local building industry. Shore stones found on the northern coast are 'foreign', carried by ice sheets from south-west Scotland, north-east Ireland, Cumbria and even the floor of the Irish Sea. An interesting display at the **Ayres Visitor Centre**, an area of raised beach, identifies the stones and their sources.

Geological processes resulted in ore deposits of lead, zinc, copper and iron which were mined at periods in Manx history. Mine workings are visible throughout the island, the greatest legacy of this industry being '*Lady Isabella*', **Laxey**'s great waterwheel, built in 1854 to pump water from the mines, and today surely the island's greatest tourist attraction.

Natural History and Wildlife

Over two-thirds of the island is in agricultural use, with good quality grassland supporting beef and dairy farming, and sheep on lowland and hill pastures. A closer look, however, will reveal many different habitats which support a rich variety of animals, birds and plants. The slate cliffs, sandy bays and coastal dunes contrast with the heather moorland, coniferous plantations, wetland and wildflower meadows.

The huge skeleton of the extinct Irish Elk exhibited in the **Manx Museum**, where the Natural History Gallery introduces the island's unique habitats, is an example of the type of giant deer found on the island when it was connected to Britain, before sea levels rose towards the end of the Ice Age. A piece of oak tree, thought to be 10,000 years old, and formerly preserved in a peat bog, is displayed at the **Wildlife Park**, **Ballaugh**, site of an ancient lake, where visitors can learn about the natural world.

Top: The view at Niarbyl
Right: A Manx cat
Below: the Snaefell Mountain Railway

Visitor Centres at the **Ayres** and **Scarlett** are operated by the Manx Wildlife Trust, who promote the conservation of natural habitats. These amenities, together with their shop at Tynwald Mills, St Johns, are most informative and will direct visitors to other nature reserves. **Ballaugh Curragh** is an area of wetland of international importance. Here, at **Close Sartfield**, 100,000 orchids bloom in the hay meadows from late May to early July and the bird hide is excellent for observing hen harriers returning at dusk to western Europe's largest winter roost. The hill land, where purple heather moorland is interspersed with golden western gorse, provides a rare habitat for hen harriers, choughs, peregrines, ravens, wheatears and skylarks. Birdwatchers will also be attracted by the variety of birds feeding in Manx waters, from the unusual wildfowl in the harbours to Britain's largest seabird, the gannet, diving for sand eels off the Ayres, where terns nest on the upper shore and lizards feed among the dunes.

The island's coastal footpath provides access to birdwatching areas. Seabird colonies are found on **Peel Hill**, **Maughold Head** and southern coasts. **Langness** is home to wintering waders and wildfowl but also a rare grasshopper found nowhere else in the British Isles. **The Calf**, the small island off the southern tip of the Isle of Man, is managed as a bird sanctuary and observatory. Day trippers arrive by boat from Port Erin or you may arrange to stay there overnight (contact Manx National Heritage for details).

Clear waters around the Calf and areas of marine conservation are rewarding for divers. Basking sharks, which can grow up to 11m (36 ft) and are harmless to humans, are sighted in Manx waters from May to August, as well as porpoises, dolphins, orca and minky whale. Boat trips offer visitors the opportunity to dive, fish or watch birds. Visitors particularly enjoy the antics of the breeding colonies of grey seals around the coastline, notably at the **Sound** and in **Peel Bay**, or catching a glimpse of the multicoloured flock of feral goats on the east coast north of **Laxey**. There are no native deer, badgers, moles, foxes or otters but walkers may glimpse an Australian wallaby, one of a feral population, escapees from the Wildlife Park, or the brown/white mountain hares. Look out for the island's own brown **Loghtan** sheep, once in danger of extinction.

The island has seventeen national glens dating from the Victorian era, many with beautiful waterfalls, where mature broadleaved trees provide a canopy for wild garlic, bluebells and a variety of fungi, and sites where bats roost and feed. Equally accessible are trails through coniferous plantations and around reservoirs owned by the Manx Government which are regularly stocked with salmon.

The profusion of red fuchsia on the hedgerows indicates the island's naturally mild climate. Look out for the only wild flower named after the island, the Isle of Man Cabbage, a yellow flowering plant found along the shoreline and a protected species because of its rarity.

Archaeology and History

The Manx landscape was exploited by the island's earliest inhabitants, who arrived about 7,500 years ago and settled along sheltered rivers and coasts, clearing the natural woodland and using the stones around them. Flint, still found on the shoreline, made tools for fishing and hunting. The prehistoric people were using the same good soils for cereal growing which today produce wheat for the island's bread.

Physical remains of the past include ancient monuments, archaeological sites and historic buildings. White quartz has been used throughout history, associated with burial practices and landmarks, perhaps indicating the special significance of this attractive stone scattered in the Manx landscape. Visitors today will discover ancient monuments dating from around 5,000 years ago and set in spectacular landscape settings. The Neolithic burial sites of **Cashtal yn Ard**, ('castle of the height') at Maughold, **King Orry's Grave** at Laxey and **Meayll Circle** at Cregneash have impressive arrangements of stone chambers. Bronze Age burial mounds are found on hill ridges and on coastal plains.

The island's geographical location has influenced its development. Its situation on sea trade routes between Scandinavia, Britain, Ireland and Europe must have been exploited from early times. Many coastal promontories have been adapted as forts, and natural vantage points used to keep 'watch and ward', a system of vigilance once maintained throughout the island. Place names reveal something of the story of the island's past. 'Barrule' means 'ward fell' and on **South Barrule** (1,585ft/483m) excavations have revealed a prehistoric hill fort enclosing 80 huts.

Little is known, however, about these early Manx people. Carved stones reveal tribal names carved in an old Irish script, Ogham, and used in the Irish Sea area. Visitors today who are interested in early Christianity will be fascinated by the Manx Crosses, the best collection being at **Maughold Parish Church**, where a monastery existed in the seventh century. Ruins of small chapels, known locally as 'keeills', named after saints and sometimes associated with ancient wells, survive in the countryside, many in spectacular settings like **Lag ny Keeilley** ('hollow of the chapel'), an isolated hermitage site on the south-west coast.

From the eighth to the thirteenth centuries the island came under Scandinavian rule. Finds today of Viking coin and treasure hoards are exciting reminders of unsettled times. The legacy of these Manx Vikings are the remains of long houses, tenth-century ornamental cross-slabs carved with runic inscriptions, and burial mounds of warriors/settlers buried with their boat, weapons, horse-trappings and possibly female sacrifice! At **Chapel Hill**, Balladoole, near Castletown, a natural plateau has provided a site for pagan and Christian burial practices, and was also used as an Iron Age fort, a boat-burial and a keeill site.

The Manx Parliament, Tynwald, shows the influence of Scandinavian ideas, deriving its name from the as-

South Barrule

sembly called the 'thing' and a Norse word meaning 'meeting place'. The tiered mound at St Johns, **Tynwald Hill**, has been used for the annual national open-air assembly of Tynwald Court for centuries.

The island's fishing grounds and minerals must have been exploited from early times. The Norse Kings of Man granted fishing and mining rights to abbeys in Cumbria, whose influence extended throughout the Irish Sea and beyond. In the medieval period the island was organised into parishes, each with a parish church named after a popular saint. These parishes still form the basis for ecclesiastical and civil life. The title of the Bishopric – Sodor and Man – reflects the extent of church and political control, with its reference to the Southern Isles of Scotland (southern from Norway). The old cathedral on **St. Patrick's Isle** reflects the island's importance in this period, as does the

establishment of **Rushen Abbey**, a daughter house of Furness in Cumbria, near Castle Rushen. Archaeological digs, ongoing at the Abbey, seek to understand this important site.

The castles at Peel and Castletown, both built at entrances to harbours, preserve evidence of occupation over hundreds of years. In Peel, displays at the **House of Manannan** include the actual replica Viking ship which made the journey of one month from Norway to the Isle of Man to celebrate the millennium of Tynwald – one thousand years old in 1979.

Because of its strategic position the island was caught up in the struggle for supremacy between Scotland and England. The kings of England prevailed over the Scots and granted the Lordship of Man to various English noblemen until it came to Sir John Stanley (ancestor of the Earls of Derby) in 1405. The Derbys, who used the flat Langness peninsula to stage their 'Derby' horse races, retained the Lordship until 1736 when it passed to the Dukes of Atholl. It was during the seventeenth century that the Isle of Man's position was exploited for smuggling purposes. Goods were landed on the island, where duties were smaller, then smuggled across to other parts of the British Isles. In order to control the loss of revenue, in 1765 the British Government revested Lordship of the island in the Crown. The Queen still retains the title 'Lord of Man'.

Seafaring was always important to the Manx economy. The presence of merchants ensured that **Castletown** had become a thriving capital with fine houses and the growth of Douglas was also assured. In the **Nautical Museum**, Castletown, a Manx-built vessel, the *Peggy*, built in 1789, is still preserved in her original boathouse. The many wrecks around the island's coasts, however, some visible at low tide and others deep under water, hold clues to the precarious nature of the its seafaring past.

Industrial development was based on the island's natural resource of water power and today there is much for the industrial archaeologist to explore. The village of Laxey now boasts two giant waterwheels plus the restored mines railway. Further mineworkings, railways, limekilns, mills and lighthouses feature in the Manx landscape.

Throughout history agriculture has remained important. People lived in dispersed rural settlements which form the basis of today's villages and towns. Place names beginning with 'balla' or ending in 'by' signify the 'home of' a particular family. The uplands used today mainly for sheep grazing were also exploited in the past. It is possible to find ancient field boundaries, the remains of round houses and old sheepfolds. Upland farms with horse-walks and tholtans (ruined cottages) were abandoned in the nineteenth century by families seeking a better living. **Cregneash** is the place where time has stood still and it is possible to experience the life of an upland village community.

Tourism became important with the introduction of regular steamship sailings in the 1830s and the growing popularity of seaside health resorts. The Victorian age produced many attractions like the splendid **Camera Obscura** on Douglas Head and the popular steam and electric railways and horse trams. The island's strong motor sport history dates from 1904.

The Isle of Man's geographical position again assured it of a role in the two world wars, when airfields, training bases and radar stations were established, and the island was used for civilian internment camps. The island's modern history has been linked to its constitutional position. Since the 1800s, when the island regained control over its finances, political control has gradually devolved from London. The island has achieved significant economic growth and Manx people today retain a sense of national identity and respect for their rich cultural heritage.

There is increasing use of the Manx language and awareness of the natural and historic environment. In the year 2000, limestone, known as 'black marble', quarried at **Poyllvaaish**, near Castletown, was used to make Millennium Crosses which may be seen around the island. In addition, the island continues to treasure its traditions. History and folklore are respected, for example, at the annual Tynwald Ceremony, where, for good luck, a sprig of bollan bane (mugwort) is worn and the path to Tynwald Hill is strewn with rushes – a tribute to Manannan.

Government and Economy

The Isle of Man is a dependent territory of the British Crown with a modern democratic government and legislature, courts and law. It has gradually developed to become largely self-governing, having responsibility for its own internal administration, financial and social policies. The British Government has responsibility for the island's international affairs and defence, and the Crown is represented by a Lieutenant Governor. The island is not part of the United Kingdom, so has no representation in either the UK or European Union parliaments. Within the European Union a special protocol guarantees free movement of products. Residents of the British Isles and of the Irish Republic do not require passports or entry visas for travel between their countries and the island.

The Isle of Man is an ancient kingdom and claims to have the world's oldest parliament, whose origins date from about one thousand years ago in the Norse Kingdom of Man and the Isles. Its membership once extended to the Scottish islands and its focus was the annual open-air assembly known as Tynwald presided over by the king, where disputes were settled and laws proclaimed. Under the rule of English lords and the Crown, Tynwald continued to meet and enact laws. The Manx National Day of 5 July, the day of the traditional open-air sitting of Tynwald at **Tynwald Hill**, is a focus of national identity.

The ceremony begins with a church service in the Royal Chapel at St. Johns with its unique seating arrangement for court procedures, and is followed by a procession of island dignitaries to the hill. Laws enacted during the year are read out in Manx and English and people have the ancient right to present petitions for redress of grievance. The ceremony is accompanied by a fair and celebration.

Throughout the year Tynwald, chaired by its President, meets in Douglas in the Legislative Chambers to decide matters of policy and expenditure. It has two branches for scrutinising legislation – the House of Keys, which has 24 elected members (general elections are held every five years), and the Legislative Council of 10 members – the island's Attorney General, the Bishop and eight members elected by the House of Keys. Tynwald was the first parliament in the world to give women the vote in 1881 and now people from the age of sixteen can vote.

The political head of the government is the Chief Minister who is assisted by the Council of Ministers, heads of government departments which are serviced by the Isle of Man Civil Service. Most of the revenue comes from indirect taxation, VAT etc. with the remainder from income tax. Local rates are administered by 24 local authorities who are responsible for their towns, villages and parishes.

Since the 1970s the island has used its unique constitutional position to develop as a low tax area and international business centre, achieving significant economic growth, with increases in population, housing and employment. The finance and supporting sectors provide major employment opportunities. Manx workers are protected by a work permit scheme, and there is little unemployment. Other employments include e-commerce, ship management and registration, engineering, manufacturing, film making and construction.

The island has experienced a considerable building programme with a new hospital, schools, prison, modern office blocks and homes, and improvements to its infrastructure in water and inland sewage treatment and roads.

Traditional employment – agriculture, fishing and tourism – continues to be important and is becoming more specialised. Farmers promote quality local produce such as locally grown wheat for Manx breadmaking, dairy products, beef and lamb. Try the delicious ice cream or award-winning Manx cheeses. Markets and farm shops offer fresh vegetables, free-range eggs, Manx honey, tomatoes and pick-your-own soft fruit. Scallops, 'Manx queenies', are an important mainstay of fishing, and the Manx kipper remains popular.

Motor sport continues to attract enthusiasts, and there is growing interest in outdoor pursuits and aspects of Manx history and culture. The island's variety of locations entice walkers, cyclists and golfers. Sheltered bays and rocky coasts are used for sailing, kayaking, fishing and diving. Tourists and residents alike respect its cultural heritage, outstanding and diverse natural beauty and quality of life.

Weather

Due to the proximity of the surrounding Irish Sea, the island's climate is generally temperate and lacking extremes found in other parts of Britain. Frosts are few and snow rarely falls. The prevailing wind direction is from the south-west. The climate varies around the island. Sea fog affects the coast at times. Rainfall and hill fog increase with altitude. Visitors should be prepared to encounter different weather conditions, sometimes within short distances. For example it may be raining in Douglas, but very often is dry and brighter in the north, away from the hills. Even on a warm day it can be surprisingly cool on the top of Snaefell or some of the other peaks, so carry extra clothing.

1. Manx Life

Why is it called the Isle of Man?

Did the island get its name from Manannan, the legendary Celtic sea god, or did he take his name from the island? Historical sources refer to Manaw, Mona, Monavia and Mon, names which appear to derive from a word meaning 'mountainous'.

Left: Wild Flowers
Opposite: Loughtan Sheep

The Manx Language

Manx Gaelic is similar to Scottish and Irish Gaelic and was spoken until the nineteenth century, when it went into decline. Today 'Manx' is taught in island schools and used at the Manx Gaelic Primary School at **St Johns.** The number of speakers is increasing. Road names appear in Manx and English. Some are translations, and sometimes the Manx is an alternative, older name. You may hear snippets of Manx on Manx Radio, the island's national radio station.

Try saying:

Moghrey mie (Morr-a my)
– good morning

Fastyr mie (Fass-ter my)
– good afternoon/evening

Oie vie (Ee-vy)
– good night

Kys t'ou (Kiss-tow)
– how are you?

Braew (Brow)
– fine

Goll as gaccan (Gull as gag un)
– goin' 'n' grumblin'

Gura mie ayd (Gurr-a-my-edd)
– thank you

Slane Lhiat (Slenn-l'yatt)
– goodbye

Many homes have Manx names. The element '*thie*' means house. The Manx word for toilet is '*thie veg*' (little house), dating from when every house had its own facility beside it!

Manx Folklore

The island has its own myths, fairy tales and folklore. Books about these are widely available. The 'little people' (*mooinjey veggey*) are acknowledged at the **Fairy Bridge** on the main Douglas to Castletown road. Fairy associations exist in place names, like Fairy Hill near Port Erin and Fairy Cottage, a station on the Manx Electric Railway, and Elfin Glen, Ramsey. Stories of supernatural creatures are associated with other locations, for example the Buggane (similar to a troll) of **St Trinian's**, a ruined church on the main Douglas to Peel road, and the Moddey Dhoo ('black dog') witnessed around **Peel Castle.**

The National Anthem

The island adopted its own national anthem in 1897, with words by W.H. Gill and sung to a traditional Manx air. The first verse:

O Land of our birth,
O gem of God's earth,
O Island so strong and so fair;
Built firm as Barrule,
Thy throne of home rule
Makes us free as thy sweet`
mountain air.

Manx Place Names

The place names of the island are composed of Gaelic and Scandinavian elements, as well as English. The word *'balley'*, of Gaelic origin, means farmstead or place, hence Ballabeg ('little farm'). The Norse work for a farmstead is *'by'*, for example Dalby ('dale farm'). The Gaelic word for mountain, *'slieau'*, is common – Slieau Managh ('mountain of the monks'), as is the Norse element *'fell'*, found in Snaefell ('snow mountain'). Douglas ('dark water') is an early Gaelic name, Ramsey ('wild garlic river') is Norse but Castletown and Peel are English names.

Most of the Manx Parishes are named after early Christian saints, some of which may be local, others common to other Gaelic areas, and some from further afield.

Manx Customs and Traditions

Certain customs are observed on the island at different times of the year. On May Eve, to protect the home, a cross of mountain ash twigs is placed above the door – look for the *'crosh cuirn'* above the door of Harry Kelly's cottage in **Cregneash**. A sprig of bollan bane (mugwort), whose magical qualities ensure protection from harm, is traditionally worn at the annual outdoor sitting of Tynwald on 5 July. Celtic New Year's Eve, 31 October, is observed with 'Hop-tu-Naa' celebrations, the lighting of turnip lanterns. The Mhelliah (harvest festival) is the highlight of the agricultural year.

The island has a rich tradition of music, song and dance. Recordings of contemporary and traditional Manx music by local groups are widely available. Find out more about Manx language and culture by visiting one of the regular festivals held in the island like **'Yn Chruinnaght'** ('the gathering'), which celebrates the traditional culture of the Isle of Man in music, song, dance, literature and arts and crafts. It attracts traditional performers and visitors from other countries.

Manx Stamps and Coins

The Isle of Man has its own stamps and currency. Only Manx stamps may be used on items posted on the island and they can be purchased at local post offices and some shops. The Isle of Man established its own independent postal service in 1973. Stamp designs have featured Manx places, events and people from history and more modern times. Issues have included stained glass windows from island churches and Harry Potter stamps to coincide with

The Isle of Man has its own currency

The Road Racing Capital of the World

The world-famous Tourist Trophy (TT) motorcycling races, held for two weeks from late May Bank Holiday, attract competitors and thousands of spectators from all over the world. The first TT race in 1905 was organised by the RAC and was for cars, with motorcycles racing from 1907. The TT Course is a demanding 37.75 miles, following the main roads from Douglas to Ballacraine near St Johns, through to Ramsey and back to Douglas over the Mountain Road the A1, A3 and A18. The lap record is less than 18 minutes! The various bends and straights are named from their location or connections, for example commemorating famous riders like Mike Hailwood or Jimmy Guthrie. These public roads and pavements are closed for practice and race sessions but it is possible to access viewing points from other roads. The TT has become a major festival, creating its own atmosphere of excitement, and includes events such as off-road trials, beach racing and rallies. Local people open their homes for 'homestay' guests and churches offer TT teas!

In late August the island hosts the Grand Prix, which attracts vintage and classic bikes. The 'Southern 100' is held on public roads around Castletown and there are regular race meetings on the old airfield at Jurby.

Island roads and tracks are also used for car rallies and kart racing. These powerful and fast races contrast with the more gracious speeds, sights and sounds of classic cars which also come to 'the road racing capital of the world' for special events.

the release of the latest film. The Philatelic Bureau in Regent Street, Douglas has further information on stamps and Manx coins.

UK notes and coins are accepted everywhere, and you will receive a mixture of UK and Manx notes and coins in your change, including Manx one pound notes! Coins have the sovereign's head on one side and interesting designs encapsulating Manx heritage on the other.

The Manx Kipper

The herring, called 'the king of the sea' in an old Manx ballad, has always been important to the Manx people. A traditional greeting would be '*palchey phuddase as skeddan dy liooar*' which translates as 'potatoes in plenty and

The TT race

'Yn Chruinnaght'

herring enough'. Salted herrings and pickled herrings were traditional Manx dishes. Delicious kippers are still produced locally at **Moore's Kipper Museum** alongside Peel harbour which dates from 1882, where guided tours are available and freshly smoked and vacuum packed kippers may be purchased or posted home. Small scallops known as 'queenies' are another Manx delicacy, which along with crab and lobster are popular in island restaurants.

A Loghtan Sheep

Loghtan Sheep

'Loghtan' is Manx Gaelic for mouse-brown which describes the colour of the fleece of this native breed of sheep, once in danger of extinction. Look out for flocks around the island, at Cregneash, the Grove Museum, Maughold Head and the Calf. The ram has four dominant curved horns and the lambs are distinctively black. Loghtan meat is a delicacy and items made from the natural wool may be purchased in Manx National Heritage shops.

Manx Cats

Most visitors want to see a Manx cat. They also ask why they have no tails. Some like the story about Noah and the pair of cats, who in Manx fashion were in no hurry to enter the ark, and made it just in time as the door closed, cutting off their tails. More likely an accident of nature, the true Manx cat is tailless, with a hollow at the end of the spine, a short body, and, like a hare, long hind legs. Variations include some without tails (rumpies) and some with short tails (stumpies). Look out for one around the towns, or visit the **Mann Cat Sanctuary** in Santon on the A5.

Manx Railways

Public Railways

With over 40 miles of vintage railways dating from the 1870s, the Isle of Man has much to interest railway enthusiasts. Whether you choose to travel north by electric or south by steam, passengers enjoy the fine country and coastal views and the freedom to alight or board, by request, along the route at a variety of stations and halts. Photographers record the unique rolling stock in action and young families enjoy the freedom of riding the different railways in the spirit of Thomas the Tank Engine. The island and its railways inspired Rev. Awdry, who based his series on the island of Sodor.

The **Steam Railway**, the longest narrow gauge steam railway in the British Isles, operates between Douglas and Port Erin, a distance of 15.5 miles, from Easter to the end of October.

Steam Train at Port Soderick

23

Journey time is 60 minutes. Use the railway to visit Port Soderick, Ballasalla, Castletown, Colby or Port St Mary. **Port Erin Railway Station** has a café and museum containing railway memorabilia.

The **Manx Electric Railway**, with its closed trams or open 'toast-racks', runs throughout the year along the east coast through spectacular coastal scenery between Douglas and Ramsey. At 17.75 miles it is also the longest of its kind in Britain. Journey time is 1 hour and 15 minutes. Use the trams to visit Groudle or Laxey, or enjoy the dramatic glens at Dhoon or Ballaglass. Tramcars numbers 1 and 2 are the two oldest working tramcars in the world! The railway opened in 1893.

At Laxey Station you change trams to ride on the **Snaefell Mountain Railway**, the only electric mountain railway in the British Isles and a superb example of Victorian enterprise. The 5 miles/half an hour's journey offers views of Laxey Wheel and, from the summit, on a clear day, of the island itself, and across the sea to England, Scotland, Ireland and Wales. The summit hotel offers refreshment and information, for example about the construction of the line. The Mountain Railway is open seasonally and is used in TT week by spectators to access the races at the Bungalow or nearby vantage points on the Mountain Road.

These railways are part of the Manx public transport system and special travel tickets allow unlimited travel on them and the buses.

Miniature Railways

Railways operated by volunteers are found at Groudle, Laxey and the Wildlife Park and are open seasonally at weekends and bank holidays. The restored Victorian **Groudle Glen Railway**, running also some summer evenings, is situated just north of Douglas and is accessible by road and from the Manx Electric Railway. It runs for three-quarters of a mile through woodland to the coastal station where a cliffside zoo once housed sea lions and polar bears!

In the Wildlife Park is the **Orchid Line**, the island's smallest passenger railway. A variety of locomotives, constructed by a model engineering society, carry passengers on a track three and a half inches wide!

In Laxey a recently restored surface section of the **Laxey Mine Railway**, built originally to haul lead and zinc, uses two working replica locomotives, the *Ant* and the *Bee*. The railway runs from the Valley Gardens, the former washing floors, to the main adit entrance. It passes through the island's longest railway tunnel under the Laxey to Ramsey road.

Horse Trams

The world's oldest surviving horse drawn tramway, opened in 1876, operates along Douglas seafront from the beginning of May to the end of September. Horses work a limited daily shift and are cared for by staff of Douglas Corporation. Signs along the promenade indicate where the horse trams will stop to allow passengers on and off. On retirement the heavy horses graze in fields at the **Home of Rest for Old Horses**, a place which welcomes visitors on the A5 south of Douglas.

The Manx Glens

The island's natural beauty is enhanced by seventeen national glens which were laid out with mainly broadleaf trees and paths in the Victorian era and are open free of charge to the public. A variety of scenery and interesting features can be explored. The gentle, wooded paths of **Glen Helen** in the west contrast with the more challenging steep steps and tracks of **Dhoon Glen** in the east, where a 500-foot descent to the shore passes magnificent waterfalls and the wheelcase, a reminder of former mine-working. **Groudle Glen** has its restored railway, while at **Silverdale** the old mill pond has become a boating lake and the playground includes a Victorian water-powered roundabout.

Bishopscourt Glen, near Kirk Michael on the A3, has a remote cave with a stone seat thought to have been used by former bishops for meditation, and at **Glen Mooar**, south of Kirk Michael, is the site of an ancient keeill (chapel) dedicated to St Patrick. The beauty of the glens changes with the seasons from the spring bluebells to the autumn fungi.

Manannan Mac Lir

Locals like to believe that the Isle of Man is named after its legendary sea god and ruler, who, in the face of invasion, hid the island under his cloak of mist and could make one man appear to be a hundred. He was a skilled navigator, understanding the weather from studying the stars, and could travel over land or sea on his horse Enbarr. On midsummer's eve people still bring their tribute of rushes to his home on **South Barrule**.

On Tynwald Day, 5 July, the path between the church and hill at St Johns is strewn with rushes as a tribute to Manannan, and on misty days Manx people will remind you that Manannan's cloak hides the island, particularly from royal visitors!

Smuggling

Manx people have always been involved in seafaring, but the island's geographical position, combined with its lower customs duties, led to it becoming in the seventeenth century what the Whitehaven customs men called 'that warehouse of frauds'! Cargoes of goods – spirits, tea, tobacco and cloths legally imported from overseas – were landed at Manx ports then smuggled across to England and Scotland, where they could be sold at a profit – as long as they escaped the notice and gunfire of pursuing revenue officers. Merchants, captains, shipowners and locals were involved in 'the trade', which became so injurious to the British Government that in 1765 they purchased the Lordship and brought the island under the British Crown.

Archibald Knox

A Manx artist and designer, born in 1864, whose work for Liberty's of London is currently highly collectable. One of the foremost designers in the English Art Nouveau movement, his designs for silver and pewter tableware, jewellery, textiles and ceramics incorporated a contemporary reworking of the type of interlace found on the Manx stone cross slabs.

Ballaglass Glen

Home of Rest for Old Horses

Horse Tram in Douglas

Silverdale Glen

Bluebells in Sulby Glen

Celtic Crosses and Scandinavian Myths

The island has a wealth of sculptured stones dating from the fifth to the twelfth centuries, many of which can be found at the churches in the parishes where they were discovered. The collection at **Maughold** includes simple inscribed and more elaborate grave memorials dating from when it was the site of an early Christian monastery. Other readily accessible collections are at **Andreas**, **Kirk Michael** and **Jurby**. Look for the slab in the doorway at St John's Church.

The art of the Manx crosses reveals many sources of influence, British and European.

The Isle of Man, in common with neighbouring Irish Sea communities, is an area of Viking settlement and influence. A remarkable number of crosses incorporate Scandinavian-style ornament and runic inscriptions and even the name of a tenth-century sculptor, Gaut, who inscribed one of his stones 'Gaut made this and all in Man'. Earlier traditions of carving stone slabs were continued by Manx Vikings and runic inscriptions bear both Celtic and Norse names showing intermarriage. Interlaced dragons are found alongside episodes from Scandinavian mythology – the Sigurd legend is a favourite. Scenes include Sigurd slaying the dragon Fafnir, roasting his heart, and licking his own fingers. An Andreas cross-slab depicts on one face a representation of the last battle of Norse mythology, when Odin is devoured by the wolf, Fenris. On the other face is a Christian figure bearing a cross.

Walks on the Isle of Man

The island is an attractive place for walkers. Large areas of hill land are open for public rambling. There is a variety of walks within a short distance, from gentle countryside lanes to the 24 peaks over 300 metres. Public footpaths are well signposted. Dogs are prohibited in some places, and in others should be kept on leads to avoid disturbance to lambs and nesting birds.

Experienced walkers are attracted by the long-distance coastal footpath, the 95-mile/153 km **Raad ny Foillan** ('Road of the Gull'), which can be tackled over a few days and using public transport, after consulting tide tables, as certain areas are inaccessible at high tide! There is also the **Millennium Way**, the 28-mile/42km ancient route

Wheel-headed Cross-slab at Lonan Old Church

through the hills linking Ramsey and Castletown, and the **Bayr ny Skeddan** ('Herring Road'), the 14-mile/22.5km fisherman's path between Peel and Castletown.

The **Steam Heritage Trail** follows the old railway track in the valley between Douglas (Quarterbridge) and Peel for 10 miles/17km.

Many shorter routes explore nature trails around the island's reservoirs, forestry plantations and glens. Towns and villages have their own heritage trails. Guide books to hill walks and long-distance footpaths and the Government's Isle of Man Public Rights of Way map may be purchased locally. The **Isle of Man Walking Festival** organises guided walks. A special event in the Manx calendar is the **Parish Walk**, when walkers, many sponsored for charity, attempt the 85-mile/135km road walk around the island's parishes!

Specialist Museums

Discover hidden treasures in the island's smaller local museums. At Peel, there is the **Leece Museum**, with its 'black hole' prison, and **Moore's Traditional Kipper Museum**, where you can experience the real aroma of kipper curing. Nearby is the **Manx Transport Museum**, where you can see the world's smallest production vehicle, the 'P50', built in Peel in the 1960s, in the island's smallest museum! The **Steam Railway Museum** in Port Erin and the **Aviation and Military Museum** near Ronaldsway Airport bring together many aspects of Manx history. All these museums are staffed by enthusiasts who are a mine of information themselves.

Walkers in the country

2. Guided Tours

This chapter will guide the visitor around the island, starting in Douglas and then exploring the north, west and south. Walks to local places of interest or good viewing points are suggested in each area, using public transport where possible. There are 600 miles of roads on the island - these are selected samples.

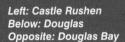

Left: Castle Rushen
Below: Douglas
Opposite: Douglas Bay

Douglas

Douglas is the capital and main port of the Isle of Man. The broad sweep of its bay, promenade and sandy beach is a classic postcard view. A closer look, however, reveals an interesting mix of Victorian and modern architecture. The splendid rows of former 'boarding houses' once accommodated thousands of factory workers from northern England who arrived by paddle steamers for their annual holidays. Today, visitors arriving on 'the boat', as Manx people describe even the fast craft operating in the Irish Sea, will find themselves in a bustling town centre. Visitors mingle with office workers and new buildings provide additional office space, shops, luxury apartments, hotels and leisure facilities. About half the island's population live in the Douglas/Onchan area but beyond the houses, on a clear day it is possible to see the surrounding countryside and **Snaefell** ('snow mountain'), the highest mountain with its radio transmission aerials, only a fifteen-minute drive away.

The main tourist information office is in the **Sea Terminal.** Buses depart from this end of the promenade/harbour, as do the horse-drawn trams running along the promenade to their terminus at the northern end near the **Manx Electric Railway Station** (known as Derby Castle). Passengers may get on or off the horse trams at designated stops along the promenade.

The Manx Electric Railway runs throughout the year to Laxey and

Ramsey. The **Steam Railway Station** is found at the inland end of the harbour. Trains run south to Castletown and Port Erin in the summer months only. Look out for details of pleasure cruises from Douglas Bay along the coast on the *Karina.*

The main shopping centre, Strand Street, is located behind the promenade, whose beautiful sunken gardens were created in the 1930s from land reclaimed from the sea. The main Post Office is found between the promenade and Strand Street, in Regent Street. To visit the **Manx Museum**, an excellent introduction to the island and where you can purchase tickets for the 'Story of Mann' sites, take Church Road beside the Sefton Hotel. It is well worth

a look inside **St Thomas's Church** as you pass – there are some murals painted by John Nicholson.

The **Gaiety Theatre** has been restored to its original 1900 décor. Designed by Frank Matchan Saturday Theatre tours offer the opportunity to see the remarkable machinery and special effects under the stage. The Theatre and **Villa Marina**, with its extensive public gardens, provide the focus for the island's arts and entertainment.

One of the earliest buildings on the seafront was the **Castle Mona.** This hotel was built as a residence in 1805 by the Lord of Man, the Duke of Atholl, using stone from the Isle of Arran. In 1963 it housed Britain's first licensed public casino.

What is the castle in Douglas Bay? Known as 'the Tower of Refuge', it was built in 1832 by Sir William Hillary. Hillary, whose bronze sculpture stands on Douglas Head overlooking the bay, organised the building having witnessed lives being lost by shipwreck on the rocks. He inspired the founding of the **Royal National Lifeboat Institution**, which provides the island with five stations. Lifeboat days and shops are well supported by the public. The lighthouses and 'herring towers', such as on **Langness** (east of Castletown on the town on the south-west corner of the island), which were visible to the fishing fleets, are another part of Manx maritime history. The one at the **Point of Ayre**, the island's most northerly building, was completed in 1818. All are now automated, the former keepers' houses providing private accommodation.

Above the harbour rises **Douglas Head**, a superb place for viewing Douglas and beyond, accessed from the south quay. Two of its buildings are **Manx Radio**, the first commercial radio station in the British Isles, and the curious **Camera Obscura**.

A Victorian curiosity, now treasured and refurbished, this fascinating building with eleven lenses and mirrors in a 'dark chamber', reflects views of Douglas Head and Bay. Prepare to be intrigued and amused. Staffed by the Victorian Society, it is open weekends in summer.

From the promenade, Victoria Street, behind the Jubilee Clock, leads to the **Library** and **Douglas Town Hall**. Look for statues of famous 'Manx' – entertainers George Formby and

Mutiny on the Bounty

Manx connections with the famous mutiny include Captain Bligh, married at **Onchan** to a daughter of a British customs officer, and Fletcher Christian who, with fellow mutineers, seized the *Bounty* en route from Tahiti in 1789 and landed at Pitcairn Island, where his descendants continued to live.

Norman Wisdom and, further on, T.E. Brown, the Manx poet. On Prospect hill are the **Government Offices** and **Legislative Buildings**, known by their design as the 'wedding cake'! Public sittings of **Tynwald** are held here and the Tynwald Library welcomes visitors. The older Douglas churches, **St Mary's** and **St George's** are located nearby.

Another road which leads to upper Douglas from the promenade is '**Broadway**' beside the Villa Marina. This leads to **St Ninian's crossroads, church** and school, **Noble's Park** and the **TT Grandstand**. This is the main area of activity during race periods, the start and finish, where bikes are prepared by mechanics, scrutinised by marshals, and refuelled. On race days the space is crammed with support teams, bike manufacturers and spectators.

To exit Douglas, there are a variety of roads. From the northern end of Douglas promenade, Summerhill Road leads to **Onchan Village** and **Onchan Park**, joining the A2 for Laxey and Ramsey, or the **Mountain Road** for Ramsey at **Governor's Bridge**. You can also access the Mountain Road from St Ninian's crossroads by continuing along Ballanard Road and taking the A21. The A11 Coast Road provides an alternative route north from Douglas promenade, via Onchan Head and **Groudle**. From the sea terminal, most traffic for the south heads over the bridge across the harbour. For Peel and the west head up Lord Street, parallel with north quay, past the red-bricked **Steam Railway Station**, and on towards the **Quarterbridge**, an important intersection and vantage point on the **TT Course**. Go straight on for Peel.

Train to Port Soderick and Coastal Walk back to Douglas via Marine Drive and Douglas Head

The combined train journey to **Port Soderick Station**, south of Douglas, and return walk of about five miles, provides the opportunity to experience the Victorian steam railway, **Port Soderick Glen**, and the amazing wild coastal scenery contrasting with the busy capital.

The twelve-minute ride passes industrial areas and wooded slopes interspersed with wild flowers, pulling gradually uphill past fields of loghtan sheep, beneath bridges and alongside rock faces, to emerge with views to the open sea. **Port Soderick Station** has waiting rooms and a small passenger car park. The 'way out' leads downhill, under the bridge to your right; follow the coastal footpath sign into the glen, continuing beside the **Crogga river**. There are a series of paths and bridges through the glen, and some natural wetland hosting 70 species of wild flowers!

Port Soderick itself contains evidence of former entertainments associated with its former use as a popular tourist resort. This peaceful, attractive cove catered for the thousands of holiday-makers who flocked to the island in Victorian and Edwardian times. You can imagine the visitors, arriving by train, electric tram or boat, strolling along the cliff walkways, enjoying the bracing sea breezes and investigating the caves. You may see the *Karina* pleasure boat which continues to ferry trippers from Douglas or even opt for a ride back. This traditional passenger vessel, included in the National Maritime Museum's register of historic ships, operates coastal cruises, with commentary, from Douglas promenade or harbour, north to Laxey and Ramsey and south to Port Soderick, Derbyhaven and Castletown.

Follow the signs from the north end of the small promenade, up a series of very steep steps, and right along the roadway, following the coastal footpath signs. An incline railway served the electric trams which ran along the coastal **Marine Drive** between here and **Douglas Head** until the 1930s. The Brooghs today, now owned by the Manx National Trust, are a stretch of dramatic headlands where birds nest below on rocky ledges and where wrecks can be spotted in the inlets far below. This walk will take a few hours, but regular seating provides opportunities to rest and savour the atmosphere. The wild flowers, particularly in the spring, are stunning. Nearby, in the bare cliffs, are strange contortions of sandstones and mudstones, millions of years old. Looking back to the south are **Santan Head** and **Langness**, with its

lighthouse and herring tower. Overhead the occasional plane prepares to land at **Ronaldsway Airport**.

The **Douglas Southern Electric Tramway** was erected by entrepreneurs, and was notable for the amount of bridgework which spanned the deep gorges. The tramway depot was at **Little Ness** headland, the limit today, because of rock falls, of vehicular access from Port Soderick. The steam power station was at **Pigeon Stream**, near the headland before you reach the arched gateway built in 1891.

The whole of **Douglas Head** was once a popular pleasure ground. Remains of an **open-air theatre** lie below the hotel, now apartments, close to the **Manx Radio** building. The panorama across the busy harbour to the quiet hills explains why it continues to be a focal point for visitors. Three

memorials on the Head have maritime connections – the Trafalgar Memorial, the statue of William Hillary, a founder of the RNLI, and a 'little piece of Whithorn' – a reminder of the tragic loss of the *Solway Harvester* in 2000.

Descend to the harbour along the roadway or down the steps beside the **Camera Obscura**, past the former **Port Skillion** open-air swimming baths. The outer harbour is where coastal tankers offload. Cross the harbour on the **Millennium Bridge**. Douglas inner harbour, with its display of yachts, is very different from the days when paddle steamers and sailing vessels moored beside the 'Coffee Palace' berth, close to the town centre and market. In the nineteenth century coffee houses were alternatives to public houses. Walk along North Quay back to the Railway Station.

North to Ramsey and the Northern Plain

Douglas to Laxey via Groudle and the Coast Road (A11 and A2)

This route follows the A11 Coast Road north from the Electric Tram terminus, roughly the same route as the railway. The first section of the railway was built in 1893 as far as **Groudle**. The stone shelter en route is a reminder that it was on these seaward looking slopes that Joseph Cunningham opened Britain's first summer holiday camp, under canvas and for men only!

The entrance to **Groudle Glen** is beside the Hotel. The miniature **Groudle Glen Railway** runs along the rocky headland to cliffs where Victorian visitors enjoyed the bracing sea air and the spectacle of a headland zoo comprising sea lions and even a polar bear! Today the railway's clifftop refreshment room is a welcome attraction. Paths follows the river inland to **Molly Quirk's Glen**.

At the junction with the A2, cross the tramlines with care – the trams whistle on approaching crossings – as there are no traffic signals. **Lonan Old Church**, named after St Adamnan, is situated about 1 mile along the first road to the right, and is one of the earliest Manx churches. A cross-slab with interlaced plaitwork stands in the churchyard and a shelter contains other fragments of crosses.

Returning to the A2 and views of the inland hills, you pass **Baldrine Methodist Chapel**. Most of the island's communities have an active chapel as well as their parish churches, very often the focus of community events, and whose buildings date from the nineteenth century. From **Baldrine**, the coastal footpath around **Clay Head** accesses the **Ballannette Nature Reserve**. In a private garden, but visible from the packhorse road behind **Garwick** stores, is an interesting stone arrangement called '**the cloven stones**', the remains of a Neolithic passage tomb.

The view of **Laxey** village unfolds. The name is Norse, describing the 'salmon river' which flows towards the harbour mouth and bay. The valley's rich source of lead and zinc ore made it the island's principal mining area in the nineteenth century. On the opposite headland you may glimpse a tram on its long climb to Ramsey.

Laxey

There is plenty to explore in **Laxey,** a historic village and mining area, only 7 miles from Douglas. Below the road bridge is **Laxey Flour Mills** (private) which has been processing Manx grain since 1861. Alongside is **Laxey Glen Gardens**, pleasure gardens, woodland and riverside paths established in the 1860s, and where there is car parking. Tram travellers change at **Laxey Station** for the **Snaefell Mountain Railway**. The rustic station and miners' church were built on the lawn of the mine captain's house, now the **Mines Tavern**.

Cross the tramlines and turn left by

the Miner's statue for **Laxey Wheel**, which stands majestically in the valley. There is a car park at the Wheel or park in Mines Road, near the Tourist Information Centre opposite **Ham and Egg Terrace**, the scenic row of miners' cottages named from the days when their residents offered teas to visitors to the Wheel. Allow ten minutes to follow the footpath across the river, where there is a picnic area, and up to the Wheel. Toilets are situated beside the river in the former powder store with its protective blast walls!

The Great Laxey Wheel

The world's largest working waterwheel stands in the Laxey valley. Driven by water power for the purpose of draining water from the underground mineworkings, the Wheel was completed in 1854 and named *'Lady Isabella'* after the governor's wife. The mines closed in 1929, but the giant wheel, 22 metres (72 ft 6 in) in diameter and 1.8 metres (6 ft) wide, and designed also as a showpiece, 'keeps turning, turning, turning', as a local folk song recalls.

The site is open for visitors from Easter to October. Those with a head for heights can climb the winding steps around the wheel's tower to the viewing platform and enjoy the wonderful views of the surrounding valley. The Mines Trail incorporates former shafts, adits, buildings and machinery – the shafts were over 2,000 feet deep! Try to work out how the wheel works, and where the water comes from! Experience the miners' damp, cramped working conditions in the re-opened underground section.

By the second half of the nineteenth century Laxey had become the greatest producer of zinc blende in the British Isles. Lead was the main product with some silver and copper. When the mines closed, the wheel was bought by a local builder and preserved as a magnificent example of engineering and industrial archaeology.

Useful information about this historical village and mining area is available from the Information Centre on Mines Road.

Other attractions in Laxey include the restored **Great Laxey Mine Railway** and another large waterwheel, newly restored and erected in **Laxey Valley Gardens**, the old washing floors where ore was processed, below the main road. At the bottom of Captain's Hill is **St George's Woollen Mill** with its traditional weaving loom producing Laxey tartan. Laxey Heritage Trail continues along Glen Road for the harbour, shore and quaint cottages of **Old Laxey**, meeting the old Douglas to Ramsey Road at the bridge by the Shore Hotel. The trail returns to the village on the other side of the river.

The tram stops at Fairy Cottage, South Cape and Minorca are convenient for access to Old Laxey and the shore.

Douglas Harbour

Tram trip to Snaefell and hike down Laxey Valley

The tram journey of about 4 miles to **Snaefell** summit takes about half an hour from **Laxey**. There are regular departures from **Laxey Station** which operate subject to weather conditions. The line opened in 1895 and was completed in just seven months, an amazing feat. The story of the construction is displayed at the **Summit Hotel**, where you can purchase refreshments and souvenirs. The journey, made in one of six original trams, is a memorable experience. The climb from Laxey provides a panoramic view of the Wheel and former mine buildings. You can imagine the extensive underground workings, where one of the shafts was deeper than the height of Snaefell! The tram usually stops or slows down for photographs.

It is a mystery why the fields across the valley have such massive walls. Areas of new tree planting give way to sheep grazing. The mountain sheep and lambs alongside the tracks seem unperturbed by the trams. Look out for unusual birds such as wheatears, stonechats and the larger hen harriers, choughs and perhaps even a sea eagle. Across the valley are the slopes of **Slieau Lhean** ('wide mountain') and the waterfall of **Glen Foss** ('waterfall glen'). In the valley bottom is the mines road which you will be walking down. Try to make out the lades above and below the track which gathered the water from the surrounding hills and channelled it for miles around the valley to be used at the mines.

At the head of the valley is **Snaefell Mine**, with the mine captain's house and smithy nearby. Sadly, twenty men died underground in 1897 in a mining accident, poisoned by carbon monoxide gas. It is difficult to imagine the harsh conditions endured by miners who walked over the hills in all weathers and then descended on ladders deep underground, with just a candle for lighting.

Shortly after passing the old power station, the tram crosses the Mountain Road, **the TT course**. The tram stops here at **The Bungalow** for passengers to alight or board. The footbridge allows people to cross the road during race periods. On the surrounding hills it is possible to see peat diggings, once the main domestic fuel. The landscape of the **Sulby Valley** with its reservoir and uplands merits designation as a National Heritage Area. It contains important wildlife habitats such as the upland heather moorland, abandoned farm buildings and extensive archaeological remains dating from up to three thousand years ago: burial mounds, round houses and shielings – huts used seasonally for tending herds grazing on hill land.

As the tram winds around the summit you experience the best views of the north and west of the island. The **Point of Ayre lighthouse** and the whitewashed **Jurby Church** to the west are landmarks. Across the sea on a clear day you can observe the Mountains of Mourne, the Mull of Galloway and Solway Firth, the Lake District and Anglesey. Views of Ramsey, North Barrule ridge, Laxey valley and over the hilltops down the east coast to Douglas complete the panorama. There is a short walk to the summit cairn and the radio transmission aerials before the journey down. What are the six kingdoms you can see?

Cross the tramlines in front of the Summit Hotel and descend to the Bungalow Station. Cross the main road carefully onto the hillside to the left of the level crossing. Follow sheep-tracks diagonlly downslope and below the main road to the **Snaefell Mine**, taking care walking beside the wide, boggy former lade. The main shaft, now capped and bearing a memorial plaque, is located beneath the wooded slope. The mine closed in 1910 but the waterwheel has been retrieved from Cornwall and Wales and re-erected in **Laxey Valley Gardens**. Some surface remains, including flotation tanks, are those of the company who re-worked the waste in the 1950s.

Down the mines road you pass a tholtan (ruined cottage) complete with pigsty, henhouse and flax mill opposite. Beside the road stands an old limekiln. There are many of these in the Manx countryside, where lime, shipped from the south of the island to the shores, was carted, burnt and spread on acidic land. Across the valley the tramline climbs up the hillside above another deserted farm called **Lhergy Veg** ('little slope'). Shortly the road reaches **Agneash** ('promontory'), a small village with farms and miners' cottages. **Agneash Methodist chapel**, opened in 1857 to serve the mining community, is still flourishing. The road continues past **Laxey Wheel** and down Wheel Hill, past the former **Mines Yard**, where you will find toilet facilities. Look for the wagon which used to haul ore from the mines and is now on display in a private garden.

The Three Legs of Man

The 'three legs' is an ancient symbol, associated, it is believed, originally with sun worship. The triple knot can be found on coins of the Norse–Irish kings of northern England in the tenth century and suggests ancestry for the Manx three legs. Its earliest use in the Island can be seen on the Maughold Parish Cross in Maughold Church, thought to date from the fourteenth century, where the legs are spurred. The Island of Sicily also has a three legs symbol. The Latin motto associated with the Manx emblem 'Quocunque jeceris stabit' translates 'whichever way you throw it, it will stand'; a reminder of Manx independent spirit and identity. The three legs is found on Manx flags in yellow on a red background, on buildings such as the Laxey Wheel, and a modern sculptured three legs appears outside the airport, commissioned in 1979 to celebrate the millennium of the Manx Parliament.

Since 1996 a new coat of arms, which is used on government buildings and can be seen in the Royal Chapel, St Johns, has featured the three legs flanked by a peregrine falcon and a raven. The falcon represents the tribute made by the Stanley family to the English kings on their coronation. The raven represents the island's Norse heritage.

Laxey to Ramsey via Maughold (A2, B11, A2, A15)

Maughold Village, on the island's north-east coast, is about 16 miles from Douglas. From Laxey continue towards Ramsey. At **Minorca** crossroads on the A2, the B11 cuts through a megalithic monument, the remains of a 5,000-year-old chambered tomb, known as **King Orry's Grave**. King Orry was a Norse ruler of the island honoured in Manx tradition, but he died on Islay! The remains of another tomb exist behind the house opposite. Did the road divide the site or were there two tombs here? Try to imagine the landscape setting of this tomb without the present houses and trees. The Manx tombs are similar to those found in Northern Ireland and southern Scotland, suggesting cultural links.

Further along the B11 in **Ballaragh**,

on the nearside hedge, is an example of ancient rock art, the **Spiral Stone**. On the opposite side a roadside stone has been inscribed by locals remembering the shipwreck of the *Merisia* steam trawler on the rocks below. The railway and coast road are very close to the cliffs at this point with views to **Maughold Head** and across to Cumbria. Look out for the feral goats on this coastline.

There is parking on the left for the **Dhoon** ('deep') **Glen**, with its steep paths and magnificent waterfalls. As you travel through the countryside you will note the lack of housing estates. The Manx Government has encouraged building within the boundaries of the villages and towns, the countryside being of high landscape value.

Half a mile further on, the road to **Port Cornaa** ('mill river') provides access to an area of rare salt marsh and stony beach, part of the Barony, a former medieval landholding belonging to St Bees Priory in Cumbria. To visit **Cashtal yn Ard** ('Castle of the Height'), the remains of a Neolithic tomb with hilltop views to the northern hills and the sea, cross the ford on the road to Port Cornaa and follow the footpath sign on the bend after Rhenab Farm.

The A2 continues through **Glen Mona**, where there is a tram stop and from where footpaths descend down through the glen to Port Cornaa or up over the hills to Snaefell. At the Hibernian crossroads the A2 continues towards Ramsey, down Slieau Lewaigue, passing Dreemskerry Road for **Maughold Venture Centre**. The minor road to the left leads to **The Gooseneck**, a famous vantage point on the TT course, passing an old road which runs along the slopes of **North Barrule** (1860 ft/ 565m) leading to **Keeill Voirrey** ('Mary's chapel') and the **North Laxey Mines**.

On the south side of **North Barrule** mountain, look for the memorial which commemorates men who lost their lives in the Manx hills, including 31 American servicemen who died in 1945 when their B-17 Flying Fortress crashed here. The memorial, marked by a flagpole, was arranged by the Manx Aviation Preservation Society who operate a fascinating museum near Ronaldsway Airport.

From the Hibernian, the A15 coast road leads to **Maughold Village**, with a diversion for **Ballaglass Glen**, charming woodland with outstanding bluebells in spring and deeply cut ravines. Soon you will have uninterrupted views of the Maughold coastline. A steep, narrow uphill road to the left leads

to the **Quakers' Burial Ground** and **Ballafayle Cairn**, another Neolithic burial site on this east-facing ridge.

Go downhill and over **Ballajora** tram crossing for Maughold Village.

Maughold Church is built on the site of an early Christian monastery and has a valuable collection of Manx crosses and, within the churchyard, examples of early keeills (chapels). Its architecture dates from the twelfth century and the fourteenth-century **Maughold Parish Cross** is unique on the island, bearing the earliest 'three legs' symbol. From Maughold Village, where there are public toilets, a road leads to **Maughold Head** and views of the lighthouse. A short, steep climb leads to the top of this former Iron Age hill fort. On the cliffs below is **St Maughold's Well**, visited locally for its healing properties.

You may park in the village and walk south, from the back of the churchyard, along the coast to **Port Mooar**, looking for seals and evidence of iron-mining trials. Another option is the walk north along **Maughold Brooghs**, between Maughold Head and **Port-e-vullen** where loghtan sheep roam and, below, the site of the island's largest cormorant colony. Other wildlife includes kittiwake, guillemot, chough, puffin and grey seals. Both coastal walks connect with the A15 to return to Maughold Village. Alternatively this coast is accessible using the trams which stop at Belle Vue, Lewaigue, Dreemskerry and Ballajora Halts.

Continuing along the A15, you will shortly have a view of **Ramsey**, with the **Queen's Pier** extending into the bay and the landmark **Albert Tower**,

41

'Karina' in Laxey Harbour

Groudle Glen

built in memory of Prince Albert who viewed the north of the island from this hill in 1847. On the roadside opposite **Port-e-Vullen** beach is a marker indicating the 1904 start of the Gordon Bennett hillclimb, the beginning of the island's road-racing history.

Douglas to Ramsey via the Mountain Road and Snaefell (A18)

This shorter, scenic route of 14 miles, unsurpassed on a fine day, with superb views of the northern uplands and northern plain, starts from the northern end of Douglas promenade. Drive up Summerhill Road, taking a left turn up Blackberry Lane. At the junction with Governor's Road, ahead, in the trees, is **Government House**, home of the island's Lieutenant Governor. Governor's Road to the right accesses Onchan Village, but turn left towards the roundabout at **Governor's Bridge**, where the Mountain Road and TT Course joins the A2.

Turn right at the roundabout, skirting the grounds of Government House and passing the growing housing estates built for the island's increasing population. At the next roundabout turn left and follow the A18 for about 14 miles to Ramsey. At **Hillberry**, the Ballacottier Road leads to the **Clypse and Kerrowdhoo Reservoirs**, available for freshwater fishing, and their rich wildlife areas. At **Creg-ny-Baa** corner the narrow B12 road leads to **Ballalheannagh Gardens**, a private development in a valley with a superb range of interesting plants.

The A18 Mountain Road is a very fast road with few speed restrictions,

Lady Isabella

so take care. It is the main route used by people from the north of the island for Douglas and the south. It is probably wise not to travel in this northerly direction in TT and Grand Prix periods when bikers tend to lap the TT course and restrictions may be in place. There are excellent views back to Douglas and the south of the Island. Place names like **Windy Corner** and **Hailwood's Rise**, named after the famous motorcyclist Mike Hailwood, indicate you have reached the highest point on the course.

The B10 branches off around the unfenced moorland towards **Barregarrow** and the **West Baldwin** valley. The **Snaefell Mountain Railway** crosses the A18 and stops here at **The Bungalow** for those who wish to ride to the top of the island's only mountain. Alternatively you may decide to walk to the top. If it is a clear day, you will be rewarded with the views of six kingdoms – England, Wales, Scotland, Ireland, the Isle of Man and the kingdom of Heaven!

From the Bungalow, the A14 descends towards **Sulby**, passing the island's largest reservoir and surrounding plantations. You can visit the site of an ancient keeill (chapel) and an abandoned farmstead on the right-hand side of the A14 just before the entrance to the reservoir. There are car parks at the reservoir and further along at **Tholt-y-Will Glen**, with a variety of exhilarating walks on offer.

The A18 continues towards Ramsey, with views down the Laxey valley from **The Verandah**, as this part of the TT course, skirting Snaefell, is known. There is parking at the lay-by known as **The Black Hut** for walkers planning to tackle the superb ridge walk to **North Barrule**. From here the A18 descends towards Ramsey, promising a breathtaking vista of the northern plain. The stone obelisk on the roadside is a memorial to Jimmy Guthrie, a TT competitor. The road bends at **The Gooseneck**.

Below the road is **Ballure Reservoir**, where the car park and picnic area provide access to reservoir and plantation walks and **Albert Tower**, the famous Ramsey landmark. Around **The Hairpin** corner is Ramsey Town. Continue straight ahead for **Parliament Square** and Ramsey shopping centre. The A2 coast road joins from the right and at the Square, the A3 and TT course connect from Peel, as does the road connecting Ramsey with the north. Parking and public toilets are nearby.

Ramsey

A local folk song evokes memories of 'Ramsey, shining by the sea'. The island's principal northern town took its name, which means 'wild garlic river', from the river mouth around which it grew. Godred Crovan, King Orry, arrived at the port in 1079 and defeated the Manx in the battle of **Sky Hill**, the wooded slope beyond the town. Look for his sculpture in the Town Hall, Library and Tourist Information Centre at Parliament Square, in the town centre.

The town centre is located south of the harbour – South Ramsey, with the town's oldest buildings, marketplace (where Saturday markets are held), shops, South Promenade, bus and Electric Railway stations. North of the harbour and connected by the stone bridge and **Swing Bridge**, built in 1892, is North Ramsey. Here is the North Promenade and **Mooragh Park**, an area of former sand dunes, river and wasteland, reclaimed in the Victorian period. The park is a superb lakeside setting of gardens and recreation area with café and toilets.

There is interesting activity around Ramsey's tidal working harbour, a mix of fishing and freight boats unloading their cargoes alongside visiting and local yachts. Cargoes arrive aboard the Ramsey Steamship Company's 'Ben' boats. *Ben* is the Manx name for girl – hence *Ben my Chree* ('girl of my heart'), the Isle of Man Steam Packet's vessel. Narrow alleys link the harbour with the main shopping street. Places to visit in South Ramsey include the Roman Catholic Church designed by Giles Gilbert Scott, who designed both Liverpool Anglican Cathedral and the red telephone box. Beside the church is the Lifeboat House and behind it, in Mona Street, are some of Ramsey's oldest properties. Much of old South Ramsey was demolished to provide the new housing, swimming pool and shops behind St Paul's Church. At the end of the South Promenade is the **Queen's Pier**, a classic Victorian pier, over 2,000 feet long, surviving from 1886 (now closed). Ramsey is known as 'Royal Ramsey' because of its royal visitors – find their names on the entrance to the pier!

Across the harbour, home to interesting wildfowl, is the shipyard where an iron-hulled sailing ship called the *Star of India*, still afloat in San Diego, California, was launched in 1863. Walk upstream, behind Ramsey Bakery, to discover **Poylldooey**, an area of rare salt marsh, nature trails and the white bridge which leads to North Ramsey and the **Grove Museum**.

To access the Grove from Parliament Square, head north across the stone bridge over the harbour and continue uphill straight ahead for less than a mile, past the **Ramsey Cottage Hospital**. Turn right just beyond the stone bridge for **Mooragh Park** and North Promenade, where oystercatchers feed on the grass beyond the houses. Ramsey's North Shore is a dune habitat, home of the rare **Isle of Man Cabbage**. From here the coastal footpath follows the shores of the northern plain.

The Grove

Situated on the outskirts of Ramsey, on the road to Andreas, the Grove was the home of Duncan Gibb, a prosperous Liverpool shipping merchant who bought a cottage here which he enlarged into a Victorian family house and summer retreat. His granddaughters preserved the vast majority of its original furnishings, fittings and family memorabilia and passed this snapshot of Victorian life to Manx National Heritage as a period museum.

Walk to Albert Tower

This walk begins at the **Hairpin** on the Mountain Road close to Ramsey. This is also the entrace to **Elfin Glen**. You may park here or walk from Ramsey town centre. Take the steps to the left of the stream and follow the stony track on **Lhergy Frissel**, a hill named after a Scottish family from Dumfries who

North Barrule

King Orry's Grave

Above: Outdoor Service at Kirk Maughold Parish Church

Right: Kirk Maughold Parish Church

Below: Mooragh Park, Ramsey

came to Ramsey in the eighteenth century and held office. The family is commemorated in Ballure church-yard, below the hill. Find your way to the Tower through the network of uphill and wooded paths. There are viewpoints through the trees near the Tower, built on the spot from where, in 1847, Prince Albert surveyed the island. Queen Victoria remained on the ship in Ramsey Bay! From the Tower retrace your steps, taking the paths down to the Mountain Road. Great care should be taken in crossing the road, where you should continue uphill, looking out for a set of wooden steps into the glen below. The planta-tion is mixed, conifer and broadleaved, with zigzag paths leading to the main road at Ballure Manx Electric Railway crossing. **Ballure** means 'place of the yew' and a large yew tree grows in the garden of Ballure Cottage. Here you may take the footpath onto the beach and return to the Queen's Pier, but this route is dependent on the state of the tide. 'Ballure Walk' is round the corner.

To return to the Hairpin, go down the road towards the town. The little whitewashed cottage is the old Ballure Inn. Turn into Walpole Road and over the tramlines. **Ballure Church** is on your left. This was the Ramsey Chapel, which went out of use when St Paul's was built, and is now private property. Its churchyard contains many notewor-thy graves including the Gibb family of the Grove Museum. The road continues past South Ramsey Bowling Club to Queen's Drive East. Turn left for Kil-leaba Mount. **Killeaba** means 'nook of the tomb' and here, in the 1960s, a burial mound used in the Neolithic and Bronze Ages was discovered. This natural mound would have had good sea views, but is now in the middle of a housing estate! From Killeaba, return via Lheaney Road then left uphill for the Hairpin or right downhill for the town centre.

The Northern Plain

Ramsey to the Point of Ayre, Bride, Jurby, Ballaugh, St Judes and Andreas (A10, A16, A10, A13, A17, A9)

The rural landscape of the **Northern Plain** is very different to that of the rest of the island. Not far from Ramsey town you will find long stretches of sandy beach accessed by a network of peaceful roads. Houses are made of shore stones, rounded by the sea, and the remote northern coasts are important areas for wildlife. Turn onto the A10 Bride Road after the Grove Museum. You will pass the **Grand Island Hotel**, a Victorian hydropathic establishment. Turn right at the roundabout in **Bride Village** for the **Point of Ayre**, 21 miles from Douglas. Inside Bride Church, named after St Bridget, is a collection of Manx crosses, including an altar front bearing graffiti – names and crosslets scratched by early Christian pilgrims.

The Point of Ayre lighthouse is the island's oldest, built in 1818. Ayre means 'gravelly bank', describing the shingle ridges which continue to form from material eroded from cliffs further south. The gravel supplies the island's building industry. Out to sea, ships pass around the island's northern tip, between Northern Ireland and north-west England. Underfoot the shingle, maritime heath and dunes provide fragile habitats for many plants, birds and insects.

The coastal footpath south-west from the lighthouse leads to the **Ayres Visitor Centre** and nature reserve. The walk is recommended – about 1.5 miles in each direction on level, grassy tracks close to the shore. **The Ayres** is excellent for birdwatching. Terns and gannets, the largest British seabird, dive for fish and grey seals follow you along the coast. Watch for porpoises, whales and dolphins but be aware of breeding birds on the shore from April to July. In August and September the Ayres is a patchwork carpet of purple heather and yellow Manx gorse.

The nearest toilets are in Bride Village, through which you will pass again as you return to the A10 to follow the coast road as far as Jurby. You will pass **Glen Truan Golf Links**, newly established in this dunes landscape. Ballaghennie road leads to the **Ayres Visitor Centre**, open most after-noons between the end of May and September. This is the first of a series of interesting narrow roads connecting with the coast which all have their own special features and where you may park and explore further.

This area is composed of glacial deposits of sand, gravel, silt and clay. Geologists study the features exposed in the northern coastline to try to under-stand the effects of the Ice Age, climate change and the movement of ice sheets across the island. The Bride Hills were formed when the ice advanced over deposits like a snowplough! The Ayres is a raised beach. Between **Phurt** and **Blue Point** is an ancient line of cliffs, which the sea once reached. On the north-eastern coast, at low tide, it is pos-sible to see the remains of a submerged forest, evidence of the times when sea level was lower.

The northern plain also has a wealth of ancient sites and evidence of prehis-toric settlement. References on maps may suggest a tumulus, round house, keeill, cairn or ship burial. Some fea-tures may be difficult to locate, not all can be seen from the road, and many are on private ground. A tumulus or cairn may indicate a burial mound, a round house could be a settlement and a keeill is the site an ancient chapel. An exciting feature of this coastline is the hilltop burial mounds dating from the Viking period – one is clearly visible at **Knock-e-Dooney**, which can be seen on the seaward skyline from the road to Rue Point. The mound con-tained a Viking warrior buried in his boat with weapons, hammer and tongs, horse and dog. A warrior's burial at **Ballateare** also contained the remains of a woman.

Blue Point today is a base for clay pigeon shooting, but all along this coast there are reminders of times past. Walls are constructed from shore stones. Old Methodist chapels, now private homes, are a reminder of times when many more people were living and working on the farms. The track next to the thatched cottage south of the Lhen

Cashtal yn Ard

Albert Tower

Ramsey Harbour

Bridge leads to **Cronk y Bing** nature reserve which is bounded by the Lhen Trench draining the extensive wetland area of **Ballaugh Curraghs**. This is a fragile and changing landscape. Coastal erosion means that the north-western coastline from **Jurby Head** down towards **Kirk Michael** is retreating. Cottages have disappeared and some buildings are dangerously near the edge of the cliff. On the beach at Jurby Head, at low tide, it is possible to see the wreck of the *Pasages*, a steam trawler from Fleetwood which ran aground in 1931.

Jurby Airfield was the site of an RAF station, whose buildings and air-raid bunkers are integrated within an industrial estate accessed from the A14. The airstrip is used for flying activities and motor sport, while nearby is the Island's prison. **Jurby Church**, dedicated to St Patrick and clearly seen from many miles around, is an island landmark. It has strong RAF connections. Manx crosses are displayed in the porch and a burial mound, possibly a ship-burial, disguised by a number of gravestones, can be found in the churchyard. Another mound overlooks the coast to the north.

Visit **Ballaugh Beach** at The Cronk, and follow the A13 through Sandygate. At St Judes crossroads follow the A17 northwards to visit the **Civil War Fort**. **Andreas Church**, dedicated to St Andrew, holds a fine display of crosses depicting stories about the heroes of Norse mythology. Turn right for Ramsey onto the A9 from Andreas Church.

Peel and the West Coast

Douglas to Peel via the Central Valley and Tynwald Hill (A1)

Peel is about 10 miles from Douglas. This route follows the **TT course** from the Grandstand on Glencrutchery Road, through the central valley on the A1, to Peel, passing through picturesque villages.

Travel in a southerly direction towards **St Ninian's Church** and School standing beside the crossroads and traffic lights, where you go straight on. There are two large secondary schools in Douglas, and one each in Castletown, Peel and Ramsey. The island's only fee-paying school is in Castletown. Bray Hill is one of the fastest sections on the TT course, and is also the location of some fine town houses. Continue straight ahead to the **Quarterbridge**, a main intersection for roads coming into Douglas. It becomes busier at main office and school run times. Turn right for Peel and the west. Alongside the road is the old railway line from Douglas to Peel, first used in 1873, now surfaced and used as an access road to the inside of the TT course when public roads are closed for racing. Walkers now enjoy the **Steam Heritage Trail** through the valley to Peel.

Continue on the main A1 to Ballacraine, about 6 miles. At **Braddan Bridge**, the road to the right leads to the island's main hospital, and a network of minor roads which access the heart of the island – the **Baldwin** valleys and **St Luke's Church**. On your left are the old and new **Braddan Parish Churches**. The roadside memorial cross is modelled on one of the crosses found here with its Scandinavian-style interlaced dragons. The old churchyard has some interesting memorial stones, including an obelisk to Lord Murray, son of a Duke of Athol, and the grave of Samuel Ally, born a slave in St Helena.

Old Kirk Braddan has a collection of early crosses and an ancient triple decker pulpit! The village of **Union Mills** is named after former corn and woollen mills. At the top of the hill is **Glenlough Farm**, a major campsite in the TT race period, with an ancient keeill site on its approach road, and beyond, the village of **Glen Vine**. The church here replaced the old **St Runius Church** which is worth exploring by taking the left-hand road, the B35, at Crosby. It has been altered but retains traces of early architecture. Half a mile south of St Runius is a group of stones bearing incised crosses. Located mysteriously in the middle of a field, this site is known as **Saint Patrick's Chair**.

At **Crosby** ('cross village') the **Millennium Way**, the long-distance footpath which follows an ancient routeway, crosses the central valley. Within a mile you will see, to your right, the ruins of **St Trinian's Church**, whose dedication to St Ninian links it with Whithorn, the Scottish monastery which once held land in this area. Mystery surrounding the history of this church is suggested by the tale of the buggane who was held responsible for its lack of a roof! **Greeba** mountain,

a Norse word meaning 'peak', rises to the north, and hidden in trees above the road is the romantic-looking home of the Victorian novelist Hall Caine.

At **Ballacraine** crossroads, the **TT course** continues to the right, northwards on the A3 via **Glen Helen**. The A3 road, left, leads to **Foxdale** and the south, passing a prehistoric ring fort and metal-working site called Port e Candas. Continue straight ahead for Peel through **St Johns**.

Tynwald Hill is where the Manx Parliament, following ancient custom, holds an open-air sitting on Tynwald Day, 5 July. This site, on a plateau surrounded by hills and close to routeways, is a natural amphitheatre and for centuries Manx people have assembled in this place. There is parking just beyond St. Johns Methodist Church at the **National Arboretum**, 25 acres of trees and lake created in 1979 to mark 1,000 years of Tynwald. The **Tynwald Exhibition** is located in the hall.

The **Royal Chapel of St John the Baptist** is a unique building. The Tynwald Ceremony begins here, where Tynwald members have personally named seats, with a church service. The arms of Lords of Man and Lieutenant Governors hang on the walls. Windows depict Christian saints from whom Manx parishes derive their dedications. In the porch is a tenth-century carved slab with Scandinavian ring-chain design and runic inscription. The processional way, past the National War Memorial, links the Church and Tynwald Hill, with its four tiers on which island dignitaries sit on 5 July.

The standing stones across the road from the church were recovered from a sandpit between here and Peel, the remains of a prehistoric burial. A massive Bronze Age burial cist remains in situ behind Tynwald Hill beside the road leading to **Tynwald Mills**, a shopping complex which includes an art gallery, the **Manx Wildlife Trust Centre** and, beside the old mill, a Manx wildflower garden open to the public. Beside Tynwald Hill is **Cooil ny Ree** and across the main road, on Old Tynwald House, a plaque on the wall commemorates the original start/finish of the 1907 **TT races**.

The wooded hill south of Tynwald Hill, **Slieau Whallian**, is traditionally pointed out as the place where witches were tried by being rolled downhill in a barrel! Historians link the tradition with other ancient Scandinavian sites where justice and punishment were meted out. The road south leads to **Foxdale**, passing the former St. John's steam railway station, where a branch line connected with the lead mines at Foxdale and tracks from Douglas split for Peel and Ramsey.

Continuing on the A1, just beyond Ballaleece bridge and farm shop, you may note the place where the steam railway passed over the road en route for Ramsey. You will soon get a view of Peel Hill and Corrin's Tower. The A1 leads past Peel cemetery and Queen Elizabeth II High School to enter **Peel.** Turn left for the harbour, **House of Manannan**, **Peel Castle** and promenade and right for **St German's Cathedral**, Peel Swimming Pool and campsite. The town centre is straight ahead.

Peel

Peel, with its quaint, narrow streets leading from the harbour and promenade, remains the most unspoilt of the Manx towns. The sea air and the waft of smoking herring evoke memories. Peel was once the home of hundreds of fishing boats and associated trades. It is easy to imagine the fishing community living in and around the sandstone cottages close to the harbour, where traditional working boats and yachts nestle beneath **Peel Castle**. Peel takes its name from the fortification built on **St Patrick's Isle**, a special secular and religious site, but is known fondly as 'sunset city', from its memorable evening skies and the fact that it has a cathedral!

The old cathedral dedicated to St. German is within the grounds of **Peel Castle**, which is accessed by the road running around the harbour, with parking at **Fenella Beach**, or by footbridge from the promenade. Buses stop on the harbour and promenade and in the town centre near the **Town Hall** and present cathedral. St Patrick's Isle has been occupied by people for thousands of years, from those living by hunting and fishing and using flint tools, to the visiting theatre companies of the present day who use the atmospheric walls as a backdrop for their productions.

Inside the castle walls are the remains of structures dating from the tenth century. The early Irish-type round tower and old cathedral with its fascinating crypt, which served as a prison, are located next to later military structures and domestic apartments. The fourteenth-century curtain walls tell the story of the castle's importance and excavations have revealed a Norse fortress, including possibly a Norse period royal or ecclesiastical palace. The castle is a major attraction revealing evidence of occupation by early Christian monks, Iron Age chieftains, Norse kings, medieval bishops and English lords and the legendary ghost of the *moddey dhoo* (black dog). This was the place where the grave of the Pagan Lady was discovered – a rich Viking lady accompanied by her cooking spit and other belongings and wearing a spectacular beaded necklace now on view in the Manx Museum. The harbour must have many stories to tell from the days of the feuding Viking kings who burnt one another's fleets. Replica Viking boats can still be seen around the harbour, perhaps taking part in a local Viking festival or crewed by office workers in the annual boat races.

The House of Manannan on the harbourside, housed partly within the original steam railway station, provides an alternative, interactive experience of the island's history, with an emphasis on its maritime past. A major exhibit here is *Odin's Raven*, the original replica Viking longship in which a mixed Norse/Manx crew rowed from Trondheim in Norway in 1979. A piece of stone from Trondheim Cathedral, carried in the ship, is on display in **St German's Cathedral**.

The father of the Norse gods, Odin, was always accompanied by two ravens, Hugi ('thought') and Munin ('memory'), who flew and brought back tidings to Odin of all they had seen or heard.

The historic centre of Old Peel is clustered around the harbour and Castle Street. There are many smuggling stories associated with this area, supposedly riddled with a maze of interconnecting underground tunnels and vaults. Further investigation today leads to the marketplace, **St Peter's Church**, interesting shops and cafés. On the harbourside are **Moore's Kipper Museum**, where kippers may be purchased or posted, the **Manx Transport Museum** (the island's smallest with limited opening hours) and Peel's own local **Leece Museum.** Visit here for '*skeet*' (news) about Peel and to see the 'black hole' vaulted prison.

There is a lovely view of Peel from the breakwater, where visitors enjoy watching the fishing, seals swimming in the bay, the lifeboat house; or take a stroll around the castle walls, whose entrance is near the kiosk and toilets.

At the northern end of the promenade, paths criss-cross the grassy headlands above the bowling green and tennis courts. Here and in the next bay were two former open-air swimming pools. These red sandstone cliffs provided the distinctive stone for Peel's buildings. A favourite walk is up Peel Hill to **Corrin's Tower** from where the views are glorious of the town and its surrounds.

Walk on Peel Hill to Corrin's Tower

This walk begins at Fenella Beach, beside the castle, and follows the footpath up the hill to the top, returning via the **Steam Heritage Trail** and River Neb, a distance of about 3 miles.

From the hill there may be sightings

of basking sharks as well as interesting seabirds. **Peel Hill** has been used by people for thousands of years. Tiny sharpened stone flint tools known as microliths, found on the hill, were used by fishermen perhaps 7,000 years ago.

The hill was once farmed. Look for old hedges and lazy beds – parallel ridges where soil was heaped up and planted with crops. As you climb, you will be rewarded with views of the beach and harbour, beyond the rooftops of old and new Peel, north along the shoreline towards Jurby, and inland through the central valley towards St Johns.

At the summit of Peel Hill is **Corrin's Tower** and a burial enclosure built in 1806 by Thomas Corrin, a nonconformist who lived below the hill, for his family. From here you can see the island's dramatic south-western coastline and southern hills.

From the tower, follow the hill track diagonally downhill and inland to the boundary wall between the hill land and fields. The path descends beside the wall. Go over the stile, marking the public footpath signed **Bayr ny Skeddan** ('the herring way'). Walk down the lane, turning left beside the red sandstone house. Follow the footpath along the farm lane and grassy lane, ignoring any field gates. The track emerges on the A27 Peel to Patrick road near **Glenfaba Bridge**.

Cross the road carefully and turn right along the pavement. After about

Lighthouse at Point of Ayre

100 yards, take the track into the **Raggatt** woodland. This interesting name suggests an ancient 'roe track' alongside the river. The place today is noted for its personal tree planting scheme. Cross the river over the bridge, turn left and join the former steam railway line. The **Steam Heritage Trail** passes **Glenfaba Mill**, and you may continue to Peel by branching onto the river path emerging near the power station. At dusk, on warm, calm summer evenings, look out for bats feeding along the River Neb. The railway station buildings are incorporated in the House of Manannan, but the water tank remains. Turn left over the bridge opposite the kipper house and back along the harbour or hill paths to Fenella Beach.

Peel to Ramsey via Kirk Michael, Ballaugh, the Wildlife Park and Sulby (A4, A3)

This route follows the A4 along the west coast to **Kirk Michael** where it joins the A3, part of the **TT course** to Ramsey, skirting the northern hills. Exit Peel by Walpole Drive at the northern end of the promenade or Christian Street from Athol Place. Soon you will be in the countryside with wonderful sea views along the coast to Jurby and across the sea to the Mull of Galloway. The steam train used to follow a similar route from St Johns to Ramsey and at certain points you will be able to make out the old tracks, now interesting footpaths, and remains of

viaducts spanning the glens.

A public footpath leads to the beach at **Lynague**, close to the sign for Cronk-y-voddy. At low tide this beach, a favourite with many visitors who once arrived by steam train, has some attractive caves. The picnic site further on is situated on a bend known as the **Devil's Elbow**. Near **Glen Mooar**, where there is access to the coast and parking, the undersea gas pipeline comes ashore, transferring fuel across the island for the Douglas electricity power station. Inland, where stone pillars once supported the railway viaduct, paths lead through the trees to **Spooyt Vane** ('white spout') waterfall. Close to the river is a keeill (chapel) site dedicated to St Patrick.

Just south of Kirk Michael Village is **Glen Wyllin** ('mill glen'), with its attractive campsite where tents may be hired, again with access to the beach and parking. The cliff line here is of interest to geologists and archaeologists. The eroding cliffs reveal evidence of glacial activity and remains of giant deer.

Opposite the entrance to Glen Wyllin is **Cooildarry** ('oak nook'), a deep wooded valley, now a Wildlife Trust Reserve, open to the public. Hundreds of flints found here suggest early occupation by humans. Visitors today can find the remains of Victorian pleasure gardens and industrial remains of a mill which used to process fuller's earth, a fine clay.

Join the **TT course** through **Kirk Michael Village**. Beyond the old castellated courthouse is the Mitre Hotel, an indication of this area's association with the Manx bishops. In the centre of the village is the parish church dedicated to St Michael. On display inside is a fine collection of cross-slabs with runic inscriptions including **Gaut's Cross**, which is 'signed' by its tenth-century sculptor. In the churchyard are the graves of five Manx bishops, who resided at **Bishopscourt**, now a private residence, about a mile north of the village, where it is possible to distinguish the fourteenth-century tower house and adjoining chapel. Take a walk in **Bishopscourt Glen** opposite, once part of the estate. It has a lake, resident wildfowl and a cave with a carved stone seat.

Inland are the Michael hills, Sartfell, Slieau Freoaghane, Slieau Dhoo and Slieau Curn. Walkers wishing to explore the hill tracks may reach them from the village via the Baltic Road near Glen Balleira. Alternatively, start near Brandywell beside Sartfell plantation on the B10, which connects the A3 at Barregarrow with the A18 Mountain Road.

Continuing on the TT course you approach Ballaugh and the famous **Ballaugh Bridge**. A detour along the A10 of about a mile leads to **Ballaugh Old Church** with its leaning gate pillars. The **Druidale** road provides an alternative route into the hills, perhaps to the hidden valley of **The Purt**, Glen Dhoo or continuing above the plantations, where hut circles and cairns on the map indicate prehistoric burial mounds, settlements and medieval shieling (summer pasture) sites.

Continuing through **Ballaugh** and **Sulby**, roads to the left access **Jurby** and the northern coastline.

Ballaugh Curraghs

Adjacent to the A3 is **Ballaugh Curraghs**, an extensive wetland, internationally important for wildlife. The area, once a huge lake, contains a rare mix of bog, scrub, woodland and hay meadows. To visit **Close Sartfield Nature Reserve**, turn off the A3 between Ballaugh and Sulby onto the B9 and take the third turning on the right, following this road for just under one mile. The reserve has a double-storey bird hide, from which panoramic views are possible of **Ballaugh Curraghs**, and boardwalks through the meadows where orchids flourish. The Curraghs are the Manx equivalent of rainforest, home to luxuriant royal ferns and wild wallabies, escapees from the nearby **Wildlife Park**!

The entrance to the Wildlife Park, which is open throughout the year, is adjacent to the A3. See endangered species from countries throughout the world and ride on the island's smallest railway, the 'Orchid Line'. From **Sulby**, site of the Royal Manx Agricultural Show in August, the A14, which climbs towards Snaefell past **Sulby Reservoir,** connects with the Mountain Road via the scenic and steep-sided **Sulby Glen**. From the A14 you may access **Sulby Claddaghs** – the name means 'river meadow land', describing this 'common land' beside the river, enclosed by the hills, and used today for camping and picnicing. The rocky outcrop above is **Cronk Sumark** ('primrose hill'), an Iron Age hill fort accessible by public footpath from the Claddagh Road, near **Ginger Hall Hotel**.

The A3 TT course continues to Ramsey through the parish of Lezayre.

Peel Castle

View from Peel Hill

Charles Street in Peel

Glen Wyllin

Just beyond its parish church is **Sky Hill**, where the **Millennium Way** begins its journey through the hills to Castletown. It was on these wooded slopes in 1079, according to the Manx Chronicles, that **Godred Crovan** hid 300 men, defeated the Manxmen, and became king, founding a dynasty of Norse kings which lasted until 1265. At **Glen Auldyn**, you pass one of the island's historic homes, occasionally open to the public. **Milntown** was the former home of the Christian family, including the Manx patriot Illiam Dhone (William Christian), who is commemorated for defending the islanders' rights in the English Civil War period.

The TT course continues right, through Parliament Square and towards the hills to begin the long climb back over the Mountain Road into Douglas.

Peel to Port Erin via the West Coast, Patrick, Glen Maye, Dalby, Niarbyl and the Round Table (A27, A36)

This route follows the A27 and the island's west coast from Peel, through the rural villages of Patrick, Glen Maye and Dalby, then climbing inland to the Round Table crossroads on the slopes of South Barrule, before descending on the A36 towards Port Erin. This route provides the best views of the island's rugged western coastline down to the Calf of Man, excellent birdwatching on moorland and coast, and magnificent views of the southern plain to Lang-

ness and Castletown. Across the water, you may see the Mourne Mountains of Northern Ireland.

Exit Peel following road signs for the south, with views of Peel Hill and Corrin's Tower to your right. Much of the island's electric power was once generated at the station below the hill. From Peel the road winds around Glenfaba Bridge, over the old railway line, and on through **Patrick Village**. This parish is dedicated to St Patrick, a popular dedication on the island, with a number of keeills, wells, and two parish churches named after him. The former parish church stands on St Patrick's Isle. The present parish church is located at the junction with the A30, the road linking Patrick with St Johns. An organic farmers' market is held along here at Ballabrooie every Thursday. Patrick Church has an unusual sundial dating from 1740, and a grave to 'some mother's son' was arranged by the music hall artiste Florrie Forde, who had a holiday cottage at Niarbyl, where his body was recovered in 1918.

At **Knockaloe** ('Olaf's Hill') farm, west of the road, now a base for Department of Agriculture advisory activities, there was a civilian internment camp throughout the First World War. It is hard to imagine that these quiet fields housed 25,000 people enclosed within an enormous compound housing their huts, exercise yards, theatres, canteens and workshops.

The three miles of coastline between Peel and Glen Maye is a popular part of the coastal footpath. At the Waterfall Hotel, **Glen Maye**, there are parking and toilet facilities. Paths lead to an amazing bridged gorge and waterfall and through the woodland to emerge at the stony beach. A wheelcase associated with former lead mines is located in the glen.

Continue towards **Dalby** where the church, supported by the local community, is the venue for the island's bonnag-making championships! Bonnag is a Manx recipe for bread without yeast. The coastline here has a series of forts, coastal defences possibly dating from prehistoric times and more recent wartime radar remains. The sign on the Ballacallin Hotel, Dalby bears the image of the Dalby spook, Gef, a talking mongoose! Find out more about this area's history at **Niarbyl** café and visitor centre. At Niarbyl, which means 'tail of rocks', there is a unique geological feature – you can stand with feet on different rocks derived from two separate continents, Africa and America. The restored thatched cottages near the beach contribute to the nostalgia of this secluded, unspoilt setting.

Continuing south, you should be able to see the Calf of Man with its stack offshore, as the road winds above the valley with its old field boundaries, up to **Dalby Mountain**. The heather moorland, heath and bogland are part of a nature reserve, with car park and footpaths. The whole area is good for birdwatching. Tracks lead north into **Glen Rushen** and southwest to **Eary Cushlin**, a coastal farm where sheep quietly graze, from where you can follow the fairly steep track to walk about a mile to **Lag ny Keeilley** ('hollow of the chapel'), an isolated hermitage site overlooking the sea.

You can see the remains of the keeill, 13 feet by 8 feet, which had an old graveyard, and on the north side, an adjoining small structure, possibly a priest's house. Grave markers with simple incised crosses have been found and artefacts from this site are on display in the Manx Museum.

To the east old mine workings are visible as the A27 continues towards the **Round Table**, an interesting name derived from a mound which is sited near this junction between old roads. A climb to the summit of the highest hill, **South Barrule**, will reveal the ramparts of a prehistoric hill fort which contains the remains of about 80 huts. This hill has commanding views of the south, but what made people live in such a defensive, inhospitable position?

The Magnetic Hill is found on the A27 about one mile south of the **Round Table** crossroads on the road to Colby. Stop your vehicle near the large white stone and you will experience the car being pulled uphill. A Manx illusion? You will be amazed!

Cronk ny Arree Laa, the summit to the west, overlooking the sea, has a massive cairn and its own modern cross-slab. Its name, which translates as 'hill of the day watch', is indicative of the value of prominent, coastal locations where locals kept 'watch and ward'. These days locals come to these moorlands in July to gather bilberries from roadside hedges!

From the descending road known as the **Sloc** ('hollow') are the best views of the south, out to Langness, the strip of land to the south-west, and along the southern coastline from Castletown to Port St Mary.

The long descent emerges at a roundabout where you may continue straight

St. Michael's Island

Silverdale Glen

Monk's Bridge

ahead, past **Rushen Parish Church** for Port Erin and Port St Mary, Cregneash and the Sound. You may turn right for **Fleshwick Bay** and **Bradda Head**. Descriptions of these places are included in the next chapter.

South to Castletown and the Southern Coastline

Douglas to Castletown via Ballasalla and Ronaldsway Airport (A5, or A6, or A25, A5)

Castletown is about 10 miles from Douglas. This route is the main one for the airport and the south. You may exit Douglas via the Quarterbridge taking the A5 south, and passing the **National Sports Centre**, **Douglas Golf Course** and expanding housing estates. This road continues to the south, passing popular attractions like the Home of Rest for Old Horses and the Fairy Bridge.

Alternatively, you may exit Douglas across the harbour bridge, passing the **Nunnery**, site of a medieval building, now a business school, before joining the main A5 at the roundabout. The narrower **Old Castletown Road**, the A25, diverts off just beyond the Nunnery, joining the A5 at the railway bridge before Ballasalla. This older and quieter road accesses the eastern coast, Port Soderick and Port Grenaugh. About a mile along this old road a footpath towards Oakhill and Kewaigue

leads to what locals suggest is the old fairy bridge. **Port Soderick** is part of the coast which may be reached by Steam Railway. At **Port Grenaugh**, a short, steep climb following the coastal footpath sign brings you to an amazing promontory fort, **Cronk ny Merriu**, with its Norse house. Further along, a road off to the left leads to the peaceful surrounds of **Santan Church** and its ancient inscribed stone slabs.

The main route south, the A5, continues from the roundabout on the outskirts of Douglas, passing the 'new' energy-from-waste plant. Prior to its opening in 2005, waste was landfilled, using former gravel pits at the Point of Ayre. The incinerator also acts as a power station, generating up to 10 per cent of the Island's electricity. The **Home of Rest for Old Horses**, run by a charity and open in summer only, is the retirement home for former tram horses and their friends who can be 'adopted'. The museum, shop and café contribute to a rewarding visit.

At **Mount Murray** there is a recent development of hotel, golf course and leisure facilities, and beyond is the **Mann Cat Sanctuary**, home to rescued animals (including Manx cats). The steam railway passes under the road, and at the bottom of the hill is the **Fairy Bridge**, where it is the custom to acknowledge the 'little people'. As the old Castletown road joins from the left, on the eastern skyline are the twin Bronze Age cairns of **Arragon**. The railway bridge here is known as the 'blackboards', dating from the days of horse-drawn traffic, when boards erected on each side of the road protected the horses from the effects of engine smoke and steam.

From this road there are superb views out to the west of the southern hills.

At **Ballasalla** ('place of the willows') you may turn right for **Silverdale Glen** and **Rushen Abbey**, the remains of a small medieval Cistercian abbey. It is possible to park at Rushen Abbey and walk upstream past the **Monks' Bridge**, a rare medieval packhorse bridge, to **Silverdale**, a charming glen with boating lake, playground and café. Alternatively there are parking and toilet facilities at Silverdale.

The Chronicles of the Kings of Man and the Isles, an important source for Manx medieval history, are thought to have been written by Cistercian monks at Rushen Abbey, near **Ballasalla.** They record that in 1134 King Olaf invited the monks of Furness to found an abbey on the island and some Norse kings were buried here. The Abbey's important role in the island's Christian heritage was marked in 2000 when

the site was bought by Manx National Heritage. Visitors can watch the 'time team' of archaeologists attempting to unravel the history of the site. A tour of the remaining buildings should include the nearby **Monks' Bridge**, only 3 feet/1 metre wide.

A left turn at the Ballasalla roundabout brings you to **Ballasalla steam railway station**, where steam trains await permission to proceed on the single track. Beyond is **Ronaldsway Airport.** This flat area, with its sheltered bay, has a long history of habitation, dating from 5,000 years ago. The name is believed to suggest the way used by the Viking King Reginald to access Castletown. Outside the airport is a unique 'three legs' sculpture. For those interested in aviation history, there is an excellent collection of memorabilia at the nearby **Manx Aviation and Military Museum**, which also tells the history of the Manx Regiment. Displays include artefacts and memorabilia relating to Manx aviation history, including the island's role in the wars for military training, the Manx Home Guard, radar sites and internment camps. The world's first area air traffic control system used by the RAF to control air space over the Irish Sea was based in Ramsey Grammar School!

King William's College, opened in 1833, with its fine buildings, is the island's only independent school. At the roundabout beyond the college you may turn left for Derbyhaven and Langness or right for Castletown and Castle Rushen. There is disc parking off the square and toilets at Castletown Civic Centre.

Douglas to Castletown via Braaid and Foxdale (A5 or A6, A24, A3)

This route through the southern uplands follows the A24, with excellent views, known as 'the plains of heaven', over the central valley and northern hills. Joining the A3 at Foxdale, the route then descends through Ballamodha towards the south.

To start, take the A5 from the Quarterbridge or the A6 from Douglas harbour to the roundabout on the outskirts of Douglas. At the roundabout head west past the business park. The Cooil Methodist Chapel is located at the next crossroads, its Sunday School opposite. About a mile further, on the right-hand side of the road, is the **Braaid Circle**, an ancient monument believed to be a farm of the Norse period. A walk down the field will reveal the remains of three buildings, one of which is boat-shaped and typical of a Norse house. Another circular building is thought to be an earlier round house.

At the next crossroads, the A26 leaves for **St Marks**, a tiny village grouped around its old church, schoolroom, Methodist chapel and smithy. Continue towards Foxdale, looking for where the Millennium Way long-distance footpath crosses this road on its journey over the hills from Ramsey to Castletown, partly on footpaths and partly on roads. The **Eairy** is a place name which signifies a 'shieling' (summer pasture). The dam, constructed to supply water for mining activity in the nineteenth century, now

attracts various species of wildfowl. **Ard Jerkell** is the headquarters of the Manx Society for the Prevention of Cruelty to Animals, and welcomes visitors.

On approaching **Foxdale** – this name does not suggest the presence of foxes, but rather comes from the Norse '*forsdalr*' ('waterfall dale') – you will notice evidence of this former lead mining area. The piles of waste material are called the 'deads'. The clock tower beside the road, built in 1901, is a proud survivor of the mining era. The new primary school is close to where a railway station was sited. The railway ran down the valley to St Johns and on to Ramsey carrying lead and returning with coal to drive steam pumps.

At the junction with the A3, as you turn left, note the miners' cottages.

The A3 continues past extensive plantations managed by the island's Forestry Department. A car park in South Barrule plantation to the right, where the A36 diverts to the west coast, gives access to peaceful forestry paths and interesting wildlife.

Follow the Ballamodha Straight as it descends south, past the entrance to **Silverdale Glen**, with its playground, boating lake and river walks.

The limestone quarries at **Billown** are the site of recent excavations which have revealed an important prehistoric landscape. Continue straight ahead at the crossroads, passing **Malew Church** before turning right at the crossroads to follow signs for car parking in Castletown. This route passes the start/finish line for the Southern 100 motorcycle course.

Castletown

The island's ancient capital has much to interest the historian, including four Manx National Heritage sites, all close to the town square. **Castle Rushen** was built in a position guarding the river and sea and the town appears to have grown up around it. Recent excavations have been carried out among the town's buildings in order to discover more about its development and trading links. The splendid medieval limestone castle is remarkably well preserved and has a long history. Its square keep dates from the time of the Norse Kings. King Magnus died here in 1265. The network of spiral staircases and parapet walk, from which there are magnificent views of the southern part of the island, belong to the fourteenth century. The castle was besieged by Robert the Bruce, became the island's centre of administration under the English Lords of Man, and was later used as a prison. The visitor experiences life in the castle through the aromas from the medieval kitchens, the magnificent rooms with their recreated furnishings, and walls where prisoners have inscribed their names. The castle, with its keep, curtain wall and glacis, is remarkably complete. The **Old House of Keys** building is beside the castle near the police station. Behind, and overlooking the sea, is the **Old Grammar School**, built as a thirteenth-century chapel. The square, home to Thursday markets, has some elegant Georgian buildings, the George Hotel, Balcony House – home of Captain Quilliam, who served on the *Victory* with Nelson – and St Mary's, the former garrison church, now offices. Quilliam's statue is located in the Speaker's garden, a restful area located within the castle's outer walls and accessible from the square and harbour. A plaque in the square commemorates the preaching place of John Wesley and the uncompleted 'candlestick' memorial – not enough money was raised for a statue – is to a former governor.

Exploration along the narrow, pedestrianised streets past old cottages, shops and cafés will reveal the delightful bowling green placed among elegant town houses. Across the harbour, scene of the annual World Tin Bath Racing championship, is the fascinating **Nautical Museum**.

In 1935 an eighteenth-century schooner-rigged armed yacht *the Peggy* was discovered in her walled-up boathouse on the harbourside at Castletown. Dating from the period of the French Revolution, the perfectly preserved vessel belonged to George Quayle, a Manx politician, scientist and inventor, who equipped it with cannons but also sliding keels for racing on Windermere in the Lake District. His eccentricities were reflected in his unique boathouse, designed with secret panels and a cabin room built like a stern cabin of the Nelson period. Visitors to the **Nautical Museum** can see the *Peggy* in its boathouse, experience Quayle's inventions and learn about the days of sail. Features include a sailmaker's workshop and items like a ship's biscuit making machine.

Coastal walk to Scarlett

For the **Scarlett Visitor Centre** and an informative coastal walk, from Castletown Square follow the signs for the narrow road past the Queen Street cottages. There is parking, seats and excellent views of Castletown and across the bay to Langness beside the flooded limestone quarry. Castletown was built from carboniferous limestone and the Centre has excellent information about this area's geology, wildlife and history.

There are some giant limekilns adjacent to the path, limestone beds containing fossils, rockpools, and, further along, a series of volcanic rocks. Look for the stack, evidence of ancient volcanic activity. Continue walking south along the coastline for about a mile, past the coastguard hut and alongside the distinctive limestone walls, hiding some interesting World War II structures. This coastal footpath passes through open, grazed fields and over steep stiles. Just before it joins Bay ny Carrickey, and **Poyllvaaish Quarry** on your

Castletown Square

The Meayll Circle

right, with its distinctive black marble, look for the ramparts of **Close ny Chiollagh**. This coastal promontory fort, excavated in the 1950s, contained a Norse-style house and, earlier, 2,000-year-old round houses. You may return the same way, or follow the public footpath signs back to Castletown or Scarlett through farmed fields.

The Southern Coastline

Castletown, Derby-haven, Langness, Port St Mary, Cregneash, the Sound and Port Erin (A12, A5 and A31)

It is worth taking time to explore the nooks and crannies of the southern coast. Footpaths follow the coastline and car parks allow access to different areas. From the airport, turn left on the A12 at the Castletown roundabout towards **Derbyhaven**, the sheltered port earlier called Ronaldsway, passing the grounds of King William's College. The Derby horse race originated here and a ruin on the right is the remains of a summer house built for the Earl of Derby. The place is known as **Hango Hill**, where Manx patriots gather annually to remember Illiam Dhone (William Christian), who was executed for his part in the Manx rebellion during the English Civil War. The port is the site of a battle in 1275 when 500 Manxmen were slaughtered.

Turn right, past former herring houses, for **St Michael's Isle**, accessed by the single track road past the hotel and golf links. Interesting buildings are **St Michael's Chapel** and **Derby Fort** of 1645 – a reminder of the Isle's strategic position. This is an excellent place to study birdlife. In fact the whole coastline from Derbyhaven to Scarlett is rewarding for birdwatchers and exciting for geologists who study the formations, dykes and fossils exposed in the limestone between Derbyhaven and Port St Mary.

Returning from St Michael's Isle and before the houses, a single track road to the left leads through the golf course to a car park from where tracks lead around **Langness** ('long nose'). The conglomerate rock arch formations are impressive. Many ships were wrecked on this coast and the herring tower was built as a landmark for shipping before the lighthouse was built in 1880.

Travelling westwards on the A5 one mile beyond Castletown, look for a signpost on the left for **Chapel Hill, Balladoole**. The lane leads to an impressive Iron Age fort, incorporating a cemetery, keeill and Viking ship-burial marked by an oval of white stones.

Continue along the coast of Bay ny Carrickey towards Port St Mary and the Sound. At the crossroads, turn left for the old fishing village of **Port St Mary.** It has some special features, including a raised walkway over the rocks, below the Town Hall. There are two piers, sheltering many yachts, and interesting buildings connected with the sea. Returning to the crossroads, turn left uphill for **Cregneash**.

Cregneash

Cregneash village, on the road from Port St Mary to the Sound, is a living museum, an example of an upland village community where time seems to have stood still. The folk museum incorporates a farm, 300 acres of natural landscape, thatched cottages, St Peter's Church, and the sheds of the wood-turner, weaver and village smithy, where traditional skills are demon-strated. Manx customs are celebrated, often with displays of Manx music and dance, and traditional farming methods are used, for example ploughing with Clydesdale horses. You can visit the home of Harry Kelly or Ned Beg Hom Ruy ('Little Ned, son of Red Tom'), hear recordings of native Manx speakers, learn about Manx folklore, or sample local food in the café next to the small shop/exhibition at Cummal Beg ('little dwelling').

This peninsula from Port St Mary around to Port Erin is known as the **Meayll** (Mull), proposed as a Manx National Heritage Area because of the nature of its historic, unspoilt landscape. Park in the Cregneash quarry car park and cross the road to follow the foot-path to the village. You may wander around the village freely, or buy a ticket to enter the buildings. You can explore the tracks on the hill behind the quarry, site of the **Meayll Circle**, a Neolithic chambered tomb. The tomb-builders chose their sites for their magnificent views. Later users of the hill, the radar operators of World War II, chose this hill to track low-flying aircraft – remains of their buildings are visible. An intriguing 'UFO' navigational aid for international aircraft is situated on the hill opposite!

A narrow road leads from the village south-east towards the **Chasms**, an interesting but dangerous feature of deep clefts in the coastline caused by ancient landslides.

Continue down the main road looking towards the **Calf**, the small island off the coast. This southern tip, called the **Sound**, 15 miles from Douglas, is the Manx equivalent of Land's End. **The Sound Visitor Centre**, specially designed to fit into the landscape, was opened in 2002. Here you can learn about the history of the Calf – the site of an early Christian hermitage – marine life and local ship-wrecks, and the work of the Calf Bird Observatory. Enjoy a meal surrounded by outstanding scenery, whilst trying to recognise the seabirds or spot the seals! Defensive ramparts remain from a pre-historic settlement and a memorial cross is a stark reminder of the many wrecks caused by the treacherous nature of the currents in the Sound. There is also a memorial to Sir Percy Cowley, whose initiative created the Manx National Trust, which owns this area and the Calf itself.

The Calf of Man

Lying off the south-western tip of the Island, the **Calf**, from the Norse '*kalfr*', indicating an islet near a larger one, is a nature reserve and bird observatory owned and managed by the Manx Government. Boat trips from Port Erin during the summer months, tide and weather permitting, allow views of seabird colonies on the cliffs and several hours to explore the island. Overnight accommodation is available, by arrangement with Manx National

Above: The Calf of Man
Left: The Soundcafe
Below: Port St. Mary

Above and Right: Port Erin
Below: Cregneash

Heritage. Resident wardens record migrating and breeding birds such as stonechat, chough, eider, storm petrel, wheatear, puffin and guillemot. The **Manx Shearwater** was first described in 1656 from a specimen found on the Calf. This bird spends most of its time at sea, coming ashore to visit its breeding burrow in summer.

Please note there are no toilet facilities for day visitors and those who stay longer should bring plenty of provisions as they may have their stay extended until weather conditions improve! However, this place is a sanctuary in many ways. It is the site of an early Christian chapel. Its peaceful atmosphere, old lighthouses, nesting birds, the bloom of purple heather in late summer, flock of loghtan sheep, and sounds of seals among the rocks, are summed up in the stone carved on the old farmhouse wall: '*parva domus, magna quies*' ('small house, big peace').

From the Sound return via the same route towards Port St Mary, with views of the whole of the southern coastline. Turn left at the crossroads for **Port Erin,** passing Port St Mary railway station, and go left at the next roundabout.

There is parking beside **Port Erin Railway Station**, which has a café and **Steam Railway Museum.** Across the road and beyond the shops is the **Erin Arts Centre** theatre. Turn left downhill for Athol Park, Breagle Glen and the lower promenade with its sandy beach and harbour, where boats leave for the Calf. There is parking and toilets in this area. Beyond is the former Liverpool University **Marine Biological Laboratory**, the first institute in the world to offer a degree in marine biology. Across the bay is **Bradda Head** and **Milner Tower**, said to be built in the shape of a key, in memory of a nineteenth-century benefactor who was a safemaker. Below the tower is a mine chimney, relic of former copper mining. Walk along the lower promenade, past St Catherine's Well and the cottages with their small gardens overlooking the shore. The upper promenade leads to **Bradda Glen**, car parking, superb southerly views and footpaths to Bradda Head.

Return to the crossroads outside Port Erin, turn left past Rushen Church, and then choose to return to Douglas via the A36, along the western coast, or on the A7 through the villages of Colby and Ballabeg to Ballasalla and the main A5 to Douglas. Look out for the steam railway or stop for a walk in **Colby Glen**.

Walk from Port St Mary over the Meayll to Port Erin

This is an interesting walk, which provides the opportunity to use public transport and visit the **Chasms** and **Cregneash**, but it will take a few hours to complete – there is so much to enjoy! The walk follows the coastal footpath, beginning at Port St Mary Town Hall, taking a right turn down the slipway to the lower promenade, and continuing to the raised walkway. Chapel Bay and Beach is named after the chapel, long disappeared, from which the Port takes its name. You will pass St Mary's Well. Walk along the raised walkway over the rocks and beside the houses, past an old boathouse, dated 1889 and alongside the inner harbour. There are some interesting buildings along this road, named 'the Underway', including a row of old cottages and a sail loft. Bear left on the Quay, past the public toilets and past the Harbour Master's House, Yacht Club and old kipper curing house. This road leads to the Alfred Pier, passing the lifeboat house and, on the pier, the Mariners' and Fishermens' Shelter in which are the names of the locals killed in 1852 during a salvage operation when the Liverpool brig *Lily*, carrying gunpowder, ran aground at the Sound.

Follow the coastal footpath sign along the walkway around Kallow Point, past the shelter where rocks form huge limestone beds containing corals. Continue along Clifton Road, and take the path beside the stone wall adjacent to the golf links. Turn left at the end of the path. Follow the coastal footpath through the private housing estate at **Perwick** towards a grassy track which leads to Glen Chass hill.

Turn left downhill and continue left along the narrow road. Soon you will enjoy the coastal views back to Port St Mary and beyond. The road becomes a track through fields in which sheep are grazing. Use stiles, keep dogs on leads and take care to close gates. At the end of the track, turn right and walk uphill through the field and gate onto higher, rough ground. The sound of choughs is a reminder of the approaching nesting sites of seabirds at the Chasms and **Sugarloaf** rock. The **Chasms** are a fascinating but dangerous series of vertical fissures in the cliffs and the Sugarloaf is a large detached rock, home to many kittiwake and guillemot. Manx National Heritage own this land and there are warnings about taking care and advising visitors to avoid climbing.

Continue uphill towards the old café building, away from the coastal footpath which continues south towards the Sound. Walk inland up a series of steps towards the top of the hill, Cronk yn Arrey ('hill of the watch'), a reminder of the necessary duties of watch and ward performed by generations of Manxmen. The building on the right was used by lighthouse keepers. On the left is an old coastguard hut. The 'UFO' is an aircraft directional beacon. From here you will have superb views down to the Sound, across to the Calf, and ahead of you, **Cregneash Village**, Meayll Hill and beyond. The road takes you through the village, where there are tearooms and toilet facilities. You will need a ticket if you wish to explore inside the buildings of this traditional Manx crofting community.

Exit the village by turning left and then take a right turn along a single track road towards Port Erin. If you have time and energy, the high ground to your right, **Meayll Hill**, is worthy of exploration. There are the remains of the radar station and the Meayll Circle prehistoric burial. The road drops steeply down towards Port Erin and brings you to the promenade. Turn right uphill for the steam railway station and buses.

The Glens

Glen	Situation	Parki
Ballaglass	Between Laxey/Ramsey	Y
Ballure Walk	Ramsey	Y
Bishops Court Glen	Between Kirk Michael/Ballaugh	Y
Bradda Glen	Port Erin	Y
Colby Glen	Colby	Y
The Purt, Glen Dhoo	nr Ballaugh	Y
Dhoon Glen	between Laxey and Ramsey	Y
Elfin Glen/ Lhergy Frissel	nr Ramsey	Y
Glen Helen	nr St Johns	Y
Glen Maye	nr Peel	Y
Glen Mooar	Between Kirk Michael/Peel	Y
Glen Wyllin	nr Kirk Michael	Y
Groudle Glen	Onchan	Y
Laxey Glen	Laxey	Y
Molly Quirks Glen	Onchan	Y
Port Soderick Glen	Port Soderick	Y
Silverdale Glen	Ballasalla	Y
Tholt-y-Will Glen	Between Snaefell and Sulby	Y
MG = Mountain Glen		
CG = Coastal Glen		

Type	Disabled Access	Remarks
MG		Valley of R. Cornaa
CG		Deep ravine to coast. Paths/picnic areas at top
MG		Good paths, lake
CG	Y	Café. Large fuchsias in upper reaches
MG		Overgrown area, but paths ok
MG		nature reserve in a remote and deserted valley
CG		Beautiful but rugged terrain
MG		Deep valley, several paths
MG	Y	Variety of glen gardens and bridges. Attractive walkways and Rhenass Fall.
CG		Spectacular waterfall
CG		White Spout waterfall nearby
CG	Y	Wooded area, campsite
CG		Valley of R. Groudle
MG	Y	Incorporates former pleasure ground and woodland planting
MG		Wooded glen, narrow in places
CG		Much to see, coastal walks
MG	Y	Woodland walks, café, water-powered merry-go-round
MG		

THE GLENS

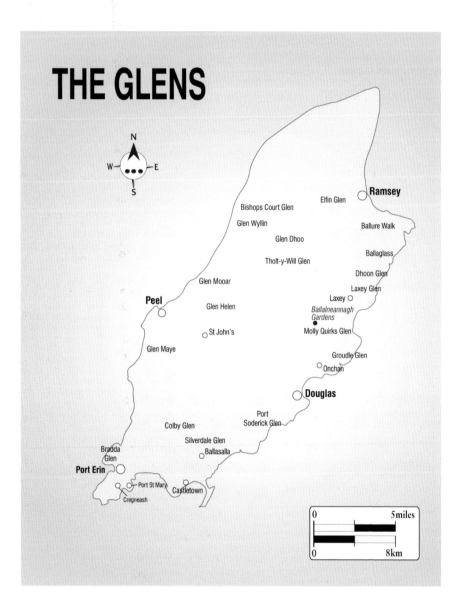

N
W — E
S

Ramsey

Elfin Glen

Bishops Court Glen

Glen Wyllin

Ballure Walk

Glen Dhoo

Ballaglass

Tholt-y-Will Glen

Dhoon Glen

Glen Mooar

Laxey Glen

Laxey

Peel

Glen Helen

Ballalneannagh
Gardens

St John's

Molly Quirks Glen

Glen Maye

Groudle Glen

Onchan

Douglas

Port
Soderick Glen

Colby Glen

Silverdale Glen

Bradda
Glen

Ballasalla

Port Erin

Port St Mary

Castletown

Cregneash

0	5 miles
0	8 km

Places to visit

Douglas

Camera Obscura

Douglas Head Road
Open: 1-4pm Sat, 11am-4pm Sun,
Easter to Sep

Gaiety Theatre

Harris Promenade
☎ 01624 620046
(Box office 694500)
Saturday theatre tours

Horse-drawn Trams

Promenade
☎ 01624 696420
Open: 9am-6pm daily, May-Sep
9am-7pm, June-Aug
Only very limited disabled access
(steps)

Manx Electric Railway

Open: daily, May-Nov
Restricted winter service
Only limited disabled access
(steps)

National Sports Centre

Groves Road
☎ 01624 688588

Nobles's Park

Nr TT Grandstand
Off Glencrutchery Road
Open: 10am-5pm, May-Sep
Disabled access

Home of Rest for Old Horses

Bulrhenny
Richmond Hill
☎ 01624 674594
Open: 10am-4pm, Mon-Fri,
May-Sep
No charge
Home for the tramway horses.
Museum, gift shop; café with home
baked cooking.

Southern Steam Railway

Douglas
Narrow gauge trains run from
Douglas to Ballasalla, Castletown
& Port Erin
Open: Daily, Apr-Nov
Limited disabled access

Manx Museum

Off Kingswood Grove
Crellins Hill
☎ 01624 648000*
Open: 10am-5pm, Mon-Sat, all year
Disabled access
No charge
Manx National Heritage HQ based
here

Villa Marina

☎ 01624 694500
Harris Promenade
Open: Gardens,
Disabled access
No charge
Outside concerts, Royal Hall (Concert
Hall)

Places to visit

Ballasalla

Rushen Abbey

☎ 01624 648000*
Open: 10am-5pm, daily, Apr-Oct
Disabled access
Modern interpretive centre and abbey ruins. Shop, herb garden.

Silverdale

☎ 01624 823474
Open: daily Easter to Sep 9am-5.30pm
Disabled access, café, playground, nature trails, craftworks studio and picnic area.

Cregneash

Sound Visitor Centre

☎ 01624 648000*
Open: Daily, summer 11am-4pm, 7-11pm Fri & Sat; winter,11am-4pm Mon-Fri; 10am-5pm Sat-Sun
Café, audio-visual presentation, glass building with turf roof. Walks, good views to Calf of Man.

Cregneash Folk Village

☎ 01624 648000*
Open: 10am-5pm, daily, Apr-Oct
Limited disabled access
A museum of rural life.

Castletown

Castle Rushen

☎ 01624 648000
Open: Apr-Oct 10am-5pm
Limited disabled access.
Medieval castle.

Nautical Museum

The Harbour
☎ 01624 648000*
Open: 10am-5pm, daily, Apr-Oct
Limited disabled access (stairs)
Home of The Peggy, an 18th century yacht launched in 1791. She was rediscovered in her boat-house in 1935 after being locked away for 120 years.

Old Grammar School

☎ 01624 648000*
Open: 10am-5pm, daily, Apr-Oct
Gift Shop
Limited disabled access (steps)
No charge
Chapel dating from 1190-1230. Converted to a school in 1701, closed 1930. Preserved as it was on its last day.

Old House of Keys

☎ 01624 648000*
Open: 10am-5pm, daily, Apr-Oct
Disabled access but step at entrance
19th century parliament building.

Manx Aviation & Military Museum

Close to Ronaldsway Airport
Open: 10am-4.30pm, weekends and Bank Holidays, Sat-Mon.
Other times by appointment.
Several exhibition rooms covering military, civil and wartime aviation.

Scarlett Visitor Centre

Castletown
Open: 2-5pm, daily, May-Sep
No charge
Limestone area, abundant wildlife and plants.

Laxey

Laxey Wheel

☎ 01624 648000*
Open: 10am-5pm, daily, Apr-Oct
Limited disabled access
Famous 25m (72ft) diameter waterwheel at old mine. Three trails and a picnic area.

Laxey Mines Railway

☎ 01624 861706
Open: Times vary
Limited disabled access
Narrow gauge railway.

Laxey Woollen Mills

Glen Road
☎ 01624 861395
Open: 10am-5pm, Mon-Sat
No charge
Limited disabled access
Working weaving mill, producing quality tartan products that are for sale.

Snaefell Mountain Railway

Open: daily, Apr-1st Oct
Limited disabled access
Electric tram to top of the mountain. 30 minute stop at the top.

Peel

House of Manannan

☎ 01624 648000*
Peel Harbour
Open: 10am-5pm, daily, all year
Disabled access and facilities.
Major tourist exhibit, built in 1997 and costing £5.5 million. It covers the island's heritage.

Leece Museum

The Old Court House
East Quay
☎ 01624 845 366
Open: 10am-4pm, Wed-Sun, Easter-Sep; 12noon-4pm, Tues-Sat, winter
No charge

Manx Transport Museum

Mill Road
☎ 01624 842448
Open: 11am-5pm, Sat, 1-5pm, Sun, Apr-Sep; Bank Holiday Mondays, 1-5pm

Moore's Traditional Kipper Museum

The Harbour
☎ 01624 843622
Open: Shop, 10am-5pm, Mon-Sat, Apr-31 Oct
Tour: as above, times may vary. Part of tour is upstairs.

Places to visit

Peel Castle

The Harbour
☎ 01624 648000*
Open: 10am-5pm, daily, Apr-Oct
Not suitable for disabled
Castle ruins on grass covered site.
Good views of Peel.

Port Erin

Port Erin Railway Museum

By the railway station
Open: 10am-5pm, daily, Apr-Oct
Large shop, two full-size steam
trains, plus carriages etc.

Breagle Glen

☎ 01624 834924
Open all year.
Bowling, tennis court and café.

Erin Arts Centre

☎ 01624 832662 (Box Office)
Open: Box Office, 1.30pm-4.30pm,
Tue-Fri; Art Exhibition, 1.30pm-
4.30pm, Tue
Music and theatre, also Sir J.
Mellon Gallery used for craft and art
exhibitions.

Niarbyl

Visitor Centre

☎ 01624 648000*
Open: 10am-4pm, daily, summer;
11am-4pm, Sat-Sun, winter
Cafe, Disabled access
Coastal site of archaeological and
geological interest.

Onchan

Onchan Park

☎ 01624 675564
Bowling, tennis, motorboating, café,
playground and stock car racing.

Groudle Glen Railway

Groudle Glen
Open: 11am-4.40pm, Sun, May-Sep;
some mid-summer evenings 7-9pm
2ft narrow gauge railway dating from
1896.

Ramsey

Mooragh Park

☎ 01624 810100
12 acre boating lake and 40 acres of
parkland with bowling green, tennis,
BMX track and playground.

Grove House & Gardens

Andreas Road
☎ 01624 648000*
Open: 10am-5pm, daily, Apr-Oct
Limited disabled access (stairs)
A Victorian time capsule.

The National Glens

Nearly half of the island is unpopulated
and uncultivated. It has led to the
establishment of 17 National glens and
other protected areas. Some of the
glens are coastal, by contrast, others
are high on the flanks of Snaefell.
Brief details of the glens are included
in this book.

Santon

Mann Cat Sanctuary

Ash Villa, Main Road
☎ 01624 824195
No charge
Alright for disabled
Open: 2-5pm, Wed-Sat, Apr-Sep;
2-5pm Sun, Oct-Mar
Gift shop, horses and ducks as well
as cats!

Bride

Ayres National Nature Reserve

North of Bride, off A10
Open: daily
Visitor Centre: 2-5pm, Tues-Sun,
May-Sep, no charge
Coastal sand dunes covering 272
hec, 670 acres

Ballaugh

Curraghs Wildlife Park

On A3 between Ballaugh and Sulby
☎ 01624 897323
Open: 10-6pm daily
(weekends only in winter)

* for information call the 'Story of
Mann' ☎ 01624 648000

What to do with children

There are plenty of opportunities for outdoor activities and learning about the environment.

Variety of beaches and glens

Sandy beaches at Douglas, Ramsey, Peel, Port Erin, Port St Mary and Laxey.

Children enjoy exploring the natural glens - the most magical and challenging are Dhoon and Ballaglass. **Silverdale Glen** has a boating lake, children's playground and craftworks.

Manx Wildlife Trust Visitor Centres

Scarlett, Castletown; and The Ayres (on the northwestern coast)
Inform about environment, plants and animals, geology etc.

Also for animal lovers

The Wildlife Park

Ballaugh
On A3
Animals and birds in walk-through enclosures, nature and butterfly trail, Orchid Line miniature railway, café, picnic area etc.

The Home of Rest for Old Horses

On A5
Feed the horses and donkeys
Café, shop and museum

Open: Weekdays and seasonally.

Ard Jerkell

Nr Foxdale on A24
(the Manx Society for Prevention of Cruelty to Animals).
Welcomes visitors to see the animals.
Café

Mann Cat Sanctuary

Santon
On A5
(Home to rescued cats (including Manx cats), horses, goats, rabbits etc.

Moaney Mooar Open Farm

Cronky Voddy, Nr Kirk Michael (signed from A3 south of Kirk Michael).

Activities

- Pony Trekking (see factfile)
- Karting at Jurby
- Children enjoy the variety of railways (see feature boxes pages)
- Swimming Pools
- National Sports Centre, Douglas (includes family fun area and café)
- Other swimming pools are at Ramsey, Peel & Castletown

Pleasure Parks

- Ramsey, Mooragh Park
  Includes children's playground, BMX track, large boating lake, tennis and crazy golf.
- Noble's Park, Douglas
  Children's playground, skateboard park, tennis and mini-golf.
- Onchan Park, Onchan
  Children's playground, motorboats, karting, mini-golf and stock cars.

Other children's playgrounds at:

Poulsom Park, Castletown (near railway station), Port Erin and Athol Park (near railway station).

Maughold Venture Centre

(signed from A2 south of Ramsey)
☎ 01624 814240
Outdoor pursuits centre

Indoors

Villa Marina

Douglas
This is the main family entertainment centre. The promenade includes: adventure play area, cinema and variety shows.
There is also another cinema in Douglas, central promenade (The Palace Cinema)

Manx National Heritage Sites

☎ 01624 648000*
Welcome families and often have special activities for children.

The House of Mananan

Peel
Has interactive features
Watch out for special events that appeal to families such as the Viking Festival at Peel.

* for information call the 'Story of Mann' ☎ 01624 648000

Please note that the dialling code from the U.K. for the Isle of Man is 01624 and this should be used to prefix Isle of Man telephone numbers.

Websites

The **Isle of Man's Department of Tourism** website gives travel information and details of accommodation, attractions, events, TT and motor sport, walking festivals, etc. Visit **www.visitisleofman.com**.

The main **Isle of Man Government** website at www.gov.im has a comprehensive index and is a mine of information.

Travelling to the Isle of Man

The island is served by air and sea from locations all over the United Kingdom. Flights connect with the English cities of Birmingham, Blackpool, Bristol, Leeds, Liverpool, London, Manchester, Newcastle and Southampton. There are also connections with Scotland via Glasgow and Edinburgh and Ireland via Belfast and Dublin. The **Isle of Man Steam Packet Company** operates ferry services from Liverpool and Heysham on the north-west coast of England and the Irish ports of Belfast and Dublin. If you are travelling to Liverpool or Heysham by rail, it may be economical to arrange combined rail and boat tickets. You may save money by booking air or sea travel online.

By air

The following airlines operate services to the island:

Aer Arann. ☎ 0800 587 2324. www.aerarran.com.

Blue Islands. ☎ 01481 727 123. www.blueislands.com.

Eastern Airways. ☎ 01652 680600. www.easternairways.com.

Euro Manx. ☎ 0870 787 7879. www.euromanx.com.

Flybe. ☎ 0871 7000 123. www.flybe.com.

Loganair. ☎ 0870 850 9850. www.loganair.co.uk.

manx2.com ☎ 08702422226. www.manx2.com

VLM Airlines. ☎ 0151 2369 696. www.flyvlm.com.

By sea

Isle of Man Steam Packet Company
☎ 08705 523 523 (UK and N. Ireland)
☎ 1800 80 50 55 (Republic of Ireland)
 www.steam-packet.com.

Ronaldsway, Isle of Man Airport is situated nine miles south of Douglas. For airport information ☎ 821600. There is a taxi rank outside the airport and car hire desks inside. Bus services operate daily to Douglas and other parts of the island.

The sea terminal is at Douglas. Taxis and bus services serving the whole Island are nearby. For ferry information ☎ 661661.

Accommodation

For information about hotels, guest houses, self-catering cottages, farm hospitality and campsites and to plan your visit, view the Department of Tourism's website at www.visitisleofman.com or contact the

Tourist Information Centre
Sea Terminal Buildings
Douglas
Isle of Man IM1 2RG
☎ 686766 or (1) 8744455 from the Republic of Ireland
fax: 627443
Email: tourism@gov.im

Opening hours: Mon-Sat 8am-7pm, Sun 10am-3pm

The Tourist Information Centre publishes a list of campsites including those with facilities for tent hire, motor caravan pitches etc., although trailer caravans are not allowed on the island without a permit.

Getting around

Ordnance Survey's Landranger map number 95 (scale 1:50,000) is invaluable for reference and information. The Isle of Man Government has its own Public Rights of Way and Outdoor Leisure Map (new digital edition), scale 1:25,000. Other maps are available, for example Harvey Maps (Superwalker), particularly useful as it shows coastline where there is no access at high tide.

The Tourist Information Centre in Douglas has a range of free leaflets and maps, including street maps which contain useful local information regarding public amenities and car hire.

By car

Driving is on the left. Road signs are in English. Any point on the island is no more than one hour away under normal road conditions, but roads in and out of Douglas may be busy at office/school opening and closing times.

There is no general island speed limit, but some stretches of road sections, and sections through towns and villages, are restricted. Free disc parking zones are signed and enforced by traffic wardens. Discs are available on board Steam Packet vessels and at the Sea Terminal, airport, vehicle hire companies, police stations and local authority offices. Seatbelts must be worn and it is an offence to use a hand-held mobile phone while driving. Petrol stations are located throughout the island.

Buses, trams and trains

Isle of Man Transport operate the island's extensive bus and rail network. Address: Transport Headquarters, Banks Circus, Douglas, Isle of Man IM1 5PT. Buses - ☎ 662525. Railways - ☎ 663366. Email: info@busandrail.gov.im.

For travel information and tickets, including economical Explorer tickets which allow unlimited travel on railways, horse tram and buses, visit the **Tourist Information/ Manx Welcome Centre**, Sea Terminal, Douglas. Explorer tickets are also on sale at main bus and rail stations. Where bus, tram or train services operate between similar places, return tickets are available that can be used for travel by either mode.

Bus services operate daily between approx. 0700 and 2300 hours, but with restricted services on Sundays and bank holidays, and connect with town centres throughout the island. From Douglas, for destinations in the south and west, buses depart from Lord Street. For the north, buses depart from Loch Promenade.

The **Manx Electric Railway** operates daily between approx. 0900 and 1700 hours from April to October (there is a more restricted service in winter). The terminus is at the northern end of Douglas Promenade, a walk of about half an hour, or can be reached by bus or horse tram. Journey time Douglas to Laxey is 30 mins. Douglas to Ramsey is 1 hour 15 mins. Change at Laxey for **Snaefell Mountain Railway** (summer season only). The last guaranteed ascent of Snaefell is at 1545; journey time is 30 mins each way.

The Steam Railway operates daily between 1000 and 1700 hours from April to October. The station is located at the end of North Quay, a ten-minute walk from the Sea Terminal. Journey time Douglas to Port Erin is one hour.

There are bus connections between the Steam Railway and Manx Electric Railway stations. The **Horse Trams**, operating daily from May to September, are a useful way of getting along Douglas Promenade ☎ 696420.

For information regarding **Groudle Glen Railway**, contact 670453 (weekends) or 622138 (evenings).

Most buses are accessible to disabled persons and arrangements can be made for disabled travellers on some railways.

Taxi, car and cycle hire

For full information, consult the **Isle of Man's Directory Enquiries Service** ☎ 118695 or the Tourist Information Centre. Taxis are available in all the main towns, but booking is advised in advance. Car hire desks are located in the Airport

Athol Car Hire ☎ 822481
Mylchreets ☎ 823533
Isle of Man Rent-a-Vehicle ☎ 825855
Cycle hire is available from Eurocycles, Douglas ☎ 624909.

Coach tours

For information, contact ProTours ☎ 674301.

Public Amenities

There are banks, cashpoints, chemists, post offices, doctors and police stations in all main towns. The main hospital is in Braddan on the outskirts of Douglas, **Noble's Hospital** ☎ 650000. **Ramsey Cottage Hospital** ☎ 811811 has a minor injuries unit open 0800 to 2200 hours daily. In case of **Emergency**, for police, ambulance, fire or coastguard, call **999**.

Local information

118695 is the **Isle of Man's Directory Enquiry Service**, for local numbers and useful information including duty chemists and road closures for motorcycling events, etc.

The **Official Isle of Man Year Book**, updated annually, and on sale at local bookshops, is a useful source of local information, listing local clubs, societies, churches, etc.

Manx Radio's website www.manxradio.com will keep you up to date with news and current affairs.

Tourist information points

The main information point is at the Sea Terminal, Douglas, ☎ 686766. For information on heritage sites, contact

Manx National Heritage
Manx Museum
Kingswood Grove
Douglas IM1 3LY
☎ 648000
www.storyofmann.com
Email: enquiries@mnh.gov.im.

For information on wildlife visitor centres, contact

Manx Wildlife Trust
Tynwald Mills
St Johns IM4 3AE
☎ 801985
www.wildlifetrust.org.uk/manxwt
Email: manxwt@cix.co.uk.

For information on arts and entertainments, performances and venues, contact the

Isle of Man Arts Council
St Andrews House, Finch Road
Douglas IM1 2HN
☎ 695598
www.artscouncil.org.im

Other informative points of contact around the island may be found at town and village commissioners' offices and public libraries who also may supply local street maps. These are listed below along with selected museum/wildlife sites which may be seasonal only. Many places have their own visitor guides, heritage trails and local information, for example about local history.

The Ayres Visitor Centre
Ballaghennie
Bride
☎ 801985

Castletown Commissioners
Civic Centre
☎ 825005

Erin Arts Centre
Victoria Square
Port Erin
☎ 832662

Laxey and Lonan Heritage Trust
Information Centre
Mines Road
☎ 862007

Laxey Village Commissioners
35 New Road
☎ 861241

Leece Museum
The Harbour
Peel
☎ 845366 (seasonal only)

Onchan Village Commissioners
Public Library
Main Road
☎ 621228

Peel Commissioners
Town Hall
Derby Road.
☎ 842341

Port Erin Commissioners
12 Bridson Street
☎ 832298

Port St Mary Commissioners
Town Hall
Promenade
☎ 832101

Ramsey Library
Town Hall
Parliament Square
☎ 810146

Scarlett Visitor Centre
Castletown
☎ 801985

Telephones

There are public telephones in most towns and villages. Phone cards for them are widely available. The Tourist Information Centre has information about mobile phones for visitors to the Island. **Manx Telecom** is the Isle of Man's telecommunications operator for fixed and mobile phones and has roaming agreements with other operators. Manx Telecom's shop is in Victoria Street, Douglas.

Weather information

There are regular news and weather forecasts on Manx Radio AM1368 or FM89, 97.2 and 103.7.

Ronaldsway Meteorological Office provides a personalised weather forecast service ideal for sailors, walkers, and golfers - for the personalised service ☎ 0900 6243 200; shipping forecast ☎ 0900 6243 322; and weather forecast ☎ 0900 6243 300.

Events

The island's culture is celebrated with a programme of events, held throughout the Island. The **Villa Marina** and **Gaiety Theatre** in Douglas are a focus for the arts, as are the **Centenary Centre** in Peel and the **Erin Arts Centre** in Port Erin. Summer concerts are held regularly in the Villa Marina Gardens and the Mooragh Park, Ramsey, and in local churches, including the Cathedral in Peel, St Thomas's Church in Douglas and St Catherine's Church inPort Erin. The **Courtyard Gallery** at Tynwald Mills Centre, St Johns, hosts exhibitions by contemporary Manx artists.

For up-to-date information contact the Tourist Information Centre or Arts Council. Local events are advertised on posters in public places, local radio, and in local newspapers - the *Examiner*, *Independent* and *Courier*, the island's free newspaper.

Main events include:

March/ April
Easter Festival of Plays
Shennaghys Jiu music festival

April
The Guild Manx music festival

May
Manx car rally

May/ June
TT Motorcycle festival
Round the Island yacht race

June
Isle of Man Walking festival
Parish Walk

Manannan Festival of Music and the Arts

July
Manx National Week
Manx Heritage Flower Festival
Viking festival
Yn Chruinnaght Celtic festival
Southern Agricultural Show
Rally Isle of Man

August
Royal Manx Agricultural Show
Jazz festival
Manx Grand Prix Motorcycle races

September
Manannan Opera festival
Bowling festival

October
Walking festival

November
Cooish Manx language festival

Leisure Facilities

Boat trips

Calf Island Cruises
Port Erin
☎ 832339

Karina Cruises
Douglas
☎ 617436 or 861724.

The main charter boat port for fishing is Port St Mary, but other boats are available from Port Erin, Douglas, Peel and Ramsey.

Gemini Charter
Port St Mary
☎ 832761

I.B. Boat Charters
Port St Mary
☎ 836028

Melissa Faye
Ramsey
☎ 813840

Useful contacts for diving are Diving Air Services and Manx Sea Charter Services
Douglas
☎ 628123

Isle of Man Sub Aqua Club
☎ 622941

The island has its own hyperbaric chamber at
Douglas Fire Station
☎ 626394.

Sailing and Yachting Clubs

Douglas Bay Yacht Club
☎ 673965

Isle of Man Yacht Club
☎ 832088

Manx Sailing and Cruising Club
Ramsey
☎ 813494

Peel Sailing and Cruising Club
☎ 842390

Fishing

Licences are available from the Tourist Information Centre, post offices and tackle shops. Rivers: for brown trout, salmon and sea trout - the season runs from 1 April to the end of September. Reservoirs: for wild brown trout and locally reared rainbow trout - the season runs from 10 March to the end of October.

Pony Trekking and Riding

Abbeylands Equestrian Centre
Douglas
☎ 676717

Ballahimmin Pony Trekking Centre
Little London
Cronk-y-Voddy
☎ 878547

GGH Equestrian Centre
the Braaid
☎ 851574

Kennaa Estate Equestrian Centre
St. John's
☎ 803039

Pennybridge Stables
Kirk Michael
☎ 878859

Quad Bikes

Quad bike trail rides
Ballacraine
St. Johns
☎ 801219

Golf Courses

Golf courses are situated at

Castletown
Langness peninsula
☎ 822220

Douglas
Pulrose
☎ 661558

Bride
Glen Truan
Ballaskilley
☎ 880359

Onchan
King Edward Bay
☎ 672709

Santon
Mount Murray Hotel and Country
Club
☎ 661111

Peel
☎ 842227
Port St. Mary
☎ 834932

Ramsey
☎ 812244

Port Erin, Rowany
☎ 834108

Port St. Mary
☎ 834932

Sports and outside pursuits

The **National Sports Centre,** Groves
Road, Douglas is the island's main
sports and leisure venue, with
swimming pool, health suite and
squash courts, etc. ☎ 688588.

Swimming pools are also located
in Ramsey, Peel and Castletown.

The Venture Centre, Maughold offers
opportunities for abseiling, canoeing,
gorge walking, etc. ☎ 814240.

For details of circular trails for cyclists
contact the Tourist Information
Centre. For mountain bikers, there
are various mountain biking trails and
there is an 'end to end' challenge in
September. ☎ 861448.

Jurby Airfield karting circuit
☎ 640050

Ayres Clay Pigeon Club
☎ 880744

Books

You will be amazed at the number of books that have been written about the Isle of Man, its people and culture. Bookshops, Tourist Information Offices and Manx National Heritage outlets, particularly the Manx Museum and House of Manannan, stock the main publications relating to the island. These cover a wide range of interests - natural history, geology, archaeology including ancient monuments, Manx crosses and the Viking Age, history including church history, industrial archaeology and transport history, constitution, Manx language, music, folklore, traditional cookery, walking and motor sport.

For information on obtaining publications by mail order, contact **Manx National Heritage,** ☎ 648000 or view the list of publications on their website, www.storyofmann.com.

Landscape, historic, cultural and motor sport videos and DVDs are also widely available and popular.

Index

Published in the UK by:
Landmark Publishing Ltd,
Ashbourne Hall, Cokayne Avenue, Ashbourne,
Derbyshire DE6 1EJ England
E-mail landmark@clara.net Website www.landmarkpublishing.co.uk

ISBN 13: 978-1-84306-162-5
ISBN 10: 1-84306-162-7

© **Marinda Fargher 2007**

British Library Cataloguing in Publication Data:
A catalogue record for this book is available from the British Library

Printed by: Cromwell Press, Trowbridge
Cartography: James Allsopp
Design: Sarah Labuhn
Edited by: This edition was updated by Ian Howe

Front cover: Laxey Wheel
Back Cover top: Point of Ayre
Back Cover bottom: The Sound

Picture Credits:
Marinda Fargher: 8, 23, 29, 42t, 47 & 50b
Isle of Man, Department of Tourism: back cover top, 6, 11, 14, 18, 19,
20, 21, 22, 26t, 26m, 27b, 28, 29, 30, 38, 50t, 58t, 64b, 67b, 71b, 70m, 71m
All other images: Jon Wornham